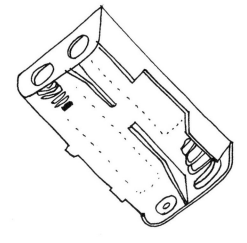

RECHARGE YOUR DESIGN BATTERIES

A RotoVision Book

Published and distributed by RotoVision SA
Route Suisse 9
CH-1295 Mies
Switzerland

RotoVision SA
Sales and Editorial Office
Sheridan House, 114 Western Road
Hove BN3 1DD, UK

Tel: +44 (0)1273 72 72 68
Fax: +44 (0)1273 72 72 69
www.rotovision.com

10 9 8 7 6 5 4 3 2 1

ISBN: 978-2-88893-048-8

Art Director for RotoVision: Tony Seddon
Design and illustration: Tonwen Jones
Typeset in Mercury Text, American Typewriter, and OPTI Morgan

Reprographics in Singapore by ProVision Pte.
Tel: +65 6334 7720
Fax: +65 6334 7721

Printed in China by 1010 Printing International Ltd.

RECHARGE YOUR DESIGN BATTERIES

Creative Challenges to Stretch Your Imagination

JOHN O'REILLY AND TONY LINKSON

RotoVision

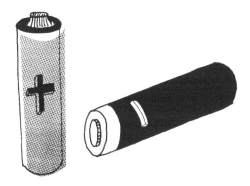

CONTENTS

INTRODUCTION

This book is called *Recharge Your Design Batteries,* but what exactly is creative energy?

Throughout history we have associated creativity with energy, from the idea of the "divine spark," to the spooky Dr Frankenstein trying to kick-start his creation, to Freud for whom "Eros" was the energy that bound impulses together into something productive. Creativity has always symbolized something powerful, whether that's a divine or a natural process. It's easy to see why creativity has been mystified over history—it is special, and it's transformative. But the basic truth is that creative people are ordinary people who make something of their experiences as a human being.

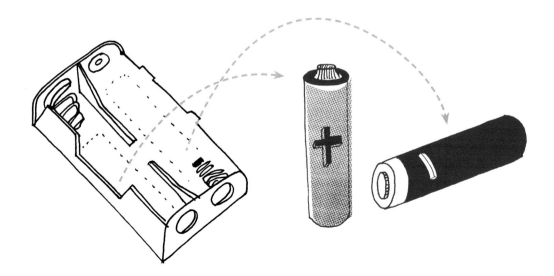

How does creative energy get used up?

It gets used up by the creative in his or her jobs because creativity is not a tool, it's not a skill, it's of who we are that can be tapped into for work, but can also be used up and burned out. One of the skills needed to be a successful creative is the ability to tap into enough energy at the right moment and then make it last for the right amount of time.

It's difficult to function effectively when running on empty. Whether it's designing, running, dancing, or playing, we all know what it feels like to get tired if we keep going without resting or feeding. The worlds of design, moving images, illustration, photography, and all the other visual communications disciplines live on the border between two essentially different territories—art and commerce. Just keeping the paycheck going can be really hard work and the belief that our jobs are an opportunity to explore some aspect of the creative spark can be submerged in the detail of earning a living.

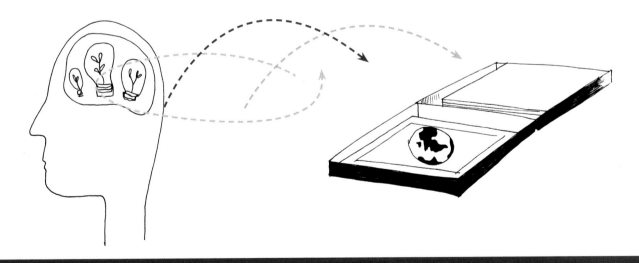

How does creative energy get recharged?

Creativity has a longer timeline than the briefs we are given to execute; it's running in parallel, always available, but the trick is gaining access. All the stories in this book are from creatives asking questions, developing new habits, exploring the creative process, using their professional skills to manage their creativity in the face of their daily professional lives. "Recharging" actually means tapping back into something that is the source of creativity. Whether you regard it as natural or divine, originating on the outside or on the inside, or a meeting of the two, creativity is something to be in contact with, to nurture a relationship with.

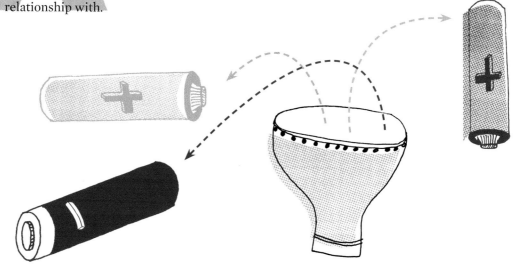

Will this book recharge my design batteries?

We've written about a series of people who have made interesting things in interesting ways. They all have a relationship to their own creativity that we thought was worth looking at. We've also written creative exercises that we hope will be helpful in some way. These exercises are not instant wisdom. They are thought-starters, ideas for entry points to different experiences of your own creativity. Picking up this book and reading it is a creative act, and you will of course make of it whatever you want.

The creative challenge is to try and make sure that, whatever our place is in the creative industries, in our work we get to build a relationship between art and commerce, between what we want and what our clients want, and between the pressure of producing work on request, and the enjoyment of being creative.

ONE:
Creative Beginnings

"An F with a G on top." The simplest, most extravagant, cheekiest beginning ever. The opening chord of The Beatles' "A Hard Day's Night." It seems to start something but then there's that gap as the chord resonates, takes its time—you can't hurry a beginning—then, at a point in time that seems to have no point, the boys start singing. It's a beginning that isn't quite a beginning. Maybe it's an opening? Or perhaps it's an introduction? It makes a mad kind of sense. Or maybe it doesn't make sense, but that doesn't matter. "An F with a G on top" is a brilliant beginning whether it makes sense or not. Creatives talk about the challenge of making that first mark, but beginning is only a problem when we see it as part of the end. It's not that we fear being tied down in some way, it's that we fear our freedom, and its creative expansc. Like The Beatles, the creatives in this section offer different approaches to beginnings, and looking at their different takes on beginnings you begin to realize that beginning really is a luxury. "An F with a G on top" was such an extraordinary beginning that some have said it was the chord that began the 1960s, a decade of new beginnings. It's why beginnings are a work in themselves, an opportunity for creative excitement, a chance to explore the beginning of the beginning.

CREATIVE BEGINNINGS:

Ian Lynam

At its simplest, the creative act comes down to one equation—the relationship between the old and the new, between executing the familiar and trying out the unfamiliar. Sometimes it is difficult to recognize when an old technique, or what was once an original idea, has outstayed its welcome and become merely an impersonation of a new idea. This is what happens in the design world when one style becomes ubiquitous and we've long forgotten the content it was attached to.

THE RED AND THE BLACK

Creatives negotiate this relationship every day. Clients often come to creatives looking for something different, namechecking a brand that was brave enough to be different. What clients really want is to be different in the same way as the brand they admire. They want the same. When it's not clients, routines and deadlines enforce the silent tyranny of the same. Often it's a change of job or role that puts us on the spot, forces us to recognize our internal resources, and compels us to mobilize them in a new way. Designer Ian Lynam had such an opportunity in 2004 when he moved to

Japan from the US. Among the vast range of clients his studio works with, across a huge variety of design disciplines, is the website Néojaponisme, of which Lynam is both art director and cofounder. Néojaponisme looks as if it is held on washy 1930s paper, complemented by painterly headline fonts in that early twentieth-century color pairing of red and black. "I was riffing off of early avant garde/modern design for the red, black, and off-white palette," says Lynam. There are echoes of the dynamic, heroic abstraction of Soviet Constructivism, and the harmony and order of De Stijl, all the while "using

This page: Illustration from 1974, a "brut collage" series depicting events, both popular and mundane, that occurred in Japan in 1974.

modern software to replicate analogue design processes."

In our digital age we mistake a plethora of tools and techniques for broader choice, when in fact it's just more tools. Part of Lynam's rationale for recreating older processes is to pare back his options, to focus, and to open up choice. "It's been really great to create a large cohesive body of work using these constraints as a system. My commercial work drifts all over the place, style-wise, so it's great to have set parameters to work within." Like the idea of Japanism or Neo-Japanism, it's about digging out a belief system, or in this case a design system.

Top left: Graphic for *The True Story of the United Red Army: the Road to Asama-Sanso*, a docudrama about the 1970s violent Japanese revolutionary goup, the United Red Army.
Top right: Illustration for Renkichi Hirato's poem "Vision".
Above: Graphic for a book review of Mieko Kawakami's *Chichi to Ran* ("Breasts & Eggs" in English).

NEO CREATIVITY

Néojaponisme is not just a visual and editorial exploration of the idea of "Japan," it also explores the concept in the context of the dynamic between new and old, the same and the different. As a country that moves in the space between the ancient and the ultramodern, Japan is a perfect vehicle for such exploration. The prefix "neo" is itself a word that insinuates itself between young and old. It's not quite new, it's certainly not "post," but "neo" means more than the simple repetition of an old style.

In the heightened language of the website's manifesto, Néojaponisme is clearly not about rejecting the past: "Although it seems tempting to demand a total annihilation of the stale cultural values of the past, the concept of scrap-and-build also seems quaintly archaic—as if the world revolves purely on change and not the choices of continuity."

The website plays with ideas of origin and originality. Sections of Japanese culture thrive on perfect reproductions of styles and fashions, one example being the Tokyo district of Harajuku, where Punks, Mods, Skinheads, Hip Hoppers, and college Preps all mix together, flaunting their styles and shopping. Néojaponisme's description of Harajuku is colorfully inspiring, but the blog also highlights the balance in this space between cultural originality, self-expression, and the marketplace.

Néojaponisme is concerned with anything that on the surface seems set in stone, whether it's a national identity or a creative methodology. They package Japan as "Japanism," reconfiguring "Japan" as a set of beliefs and ideas that are attached to cultural styles and practices by all of us, whether we're Japanese or outsiders fascinated by the culture or the "trendcentral" idea that dominates marketing and journalism. Lynam's treatment of photography puts these images of Japan into question, suggesting that we shouldn't take them at their face value or fetishize them. He doesn't hide the image, he reframes it, painting over it, "tearing" it along the edge. "Neo" as a design style gives images "a point of view."

Far left: Illustration from the 1974 series.
Left: Illustration to accompany an interview with Japanese architect Keiji Ashizawa.

THE NEW AND THE ORIGINAL

After switching continents, Lynam has had to adapt his creative eye to find this point of view. "I enjoy errant lines more now, particularly in pattern design. I used to be really anal about drawing all vectors properly, according to how PostScript works, but I've thrown that to the wind and I've been enjoying chance processes a lot more."

Going back to a familiar source in avant garde design and exploring its possibilities anew makes sense—it's both an anchor and a platform for seeing things. "Integrating [Japanese] typography with my western typography has been a huge learning process. Being forced to start over and essentially learn a gigantic aspect of your profession again from another cultural angle has been great. I definitely think of space more rhythmically due to designing with kanji and kana."

Lynam's creative practice has also been inspired by a different awareness of the power of the symbolic, and how the deep cultural values we attach to certain kinds of images are very relative but no less powerful: "I've learned a lot about the localized visual symbolism and iconography that is used in design here a lot more than elsewhere in the world. The biggest example I can think of is the 'sprouting plant shape.' I swear there are at least 100 corporations here milking that idea for all it's worth."

Individually, there are practices and ways of thinking that we hang on to; that's fine, but when they remain unexamined they can become frozen, their original use and purpose forgotten. It's what happens when an original design idea becomes a "style," to be wheeled out again and again. Old ways of thinking and doing things become safe and secure, an end in themselves rather than a means to an end. Inspiration is about finding and creating a different channel between the old and the new, between continuity and discontinuity, between the skills and knowledge we rely on and the unknown places we need to push them toward. And though we often see change as an end in itself, change is about the beginning, not the end.

The challenge for the creative is to find a way to break out of the passive inertia of the tried and tested. And the idea of the "neo" is one way of doing that. Applying the "neo" as a creative strategy in your work is a simple and inspiring game to play. It allows you to continue what you are doing while giving you a new framework in which to do it. It allows you to see your own creative practices, or a client's brand values, as ideas that are no longer set in stone.

Above: Accompanying graphic to an interview with Sumie Kawakami, author of the book *Goodbye Madame Butterfly: Sex, Marriage and the Modern Japanese Woman*.

WHY NOT TRY...

Playing with a new version of an old design style, look, or font. Twist it, stretch it, turn it inside out, and create your own reading of a moment in design history. Play with it as a new belief system....neo-helveticism?! Our working lives are spent creating, evolving, or maintaining a coherent set of beliefs and ideas for others—for clients and brands. Try playing with some of your own.

SKETCHBOOK:
Alfalfa Studio

Every artist needs a safe space in which to begin a creative project. Creative beginnings can abruptly come to an end if they aren't cared for sufficiently. The sketchbook has proved to be the enduring companion for the artist. The portable pages offer a private space for recording sudden inspirations, mad plans, raw thoughts, drawings, trials and experiments, and the seeds of what can become fully grown projects if well looked after. Rafael Esquer of Alfalfa Studio says, "Sketching is an important creative activity for me. In fact, for more than a decade I've kept a sketchbook where I draw, write, paste, and experiment on an almost daily basis. I have a stack of dozens of them."

Below: Esquer's sketchbook in his New York studio.
Opposite page: Examples of sketches inspired by Esquer's passion for Mexico, as well as his current life in New York.

POWER OF PLACE

Though Esquer lives and works in New York City, he originates from Mexico, which is as Esquer tells us, a place that has "never been known for its industrial achievements, technological wizardry, or economical powers. It is rather known for its poets, philosophers, writers, revolutionaries, and artists." He has filled many sketchbooks with his passion for Mexico, books in which "you will find traces of mystery that not only represent who I am but express something of the essence of my homeland." Esquer uses his sketchbooks to make contact with a place he doesn't live anymore. He reaches out with his drawing, writing, pasting, and experimenting, stretching himself creatively in order to remain connected. He continues, "My 'day-by-day' sketchbook is at once a journal, a source, and a creative repository. It is where ideas are born and deposited at the end of every day. It is where my Mexicanness lives, my inspiration, my happiness, and my frustration. It is where I become México, a writer, a poet, a philosopher, a revolutionary, an explorer, a lover, an artist, a designer."

Esquer is clearly inspired by his homeland, and the riches of Mexico make that entirely understandable. Inspiration can also come from, and go to, many other places. There are the expected ones: studios, universities and art schools, museums and galleries, movies and theater, and then there's the places in between urbanity and nature, inside and outside; buses, trains, bathroom sinks, in front of a can of beans in the supermarket, or in front of the TV. All of these places can be the place where inspiration strikes. It's good to get out and have an experience.

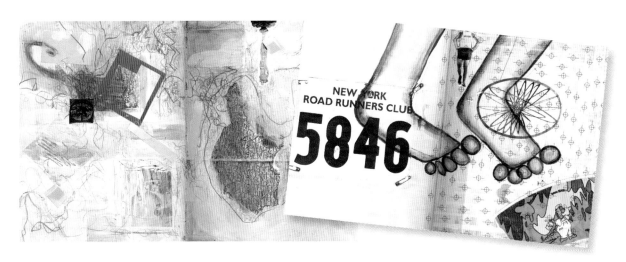

SEE-THROUGH INSPIRATION

The renowned American architect Philip Johnson worked extensively with glass in his early career. His 1949 masterpiece was his home, the Glass House, situated within his grounds at the edge of a crest overlooking a pond in New Canaan, Connecticut. The building's sides are almost all glass, making the rich exterior view its dominant visual experience.

Johnson died in 2005. In the summer of 2007, Esquer was commissioned to document the historic Civic and Gala Opening of The Philip Johnson Glass House, which is now a site of the National Trust for Historic Preservation and open to the public for tours. Esquer filmed interviews with guests such as modernist architecture photographer Julius Shulman, *The New Yorker*'s architectural critic Paul

Golderberger, Eames Demetrios, graphic designer Carin Goldberg, and architects Fred Noyes, Calvin Tsao, and Craig Bassam, among others. The result was a collection of three short films entitled *Glass House Openings* that collectively captured the inspired reflections from these guests who had attended the opening. The third film *The Power of Place* was the inspiration for and the literal ingredients of Esquer's response to a brief from Moleskine®/Glass House who commissioned 29 sketches from a variety of designers, architects, and artists to fill a custom book called *The Glass House Sketchbook*. Esquer explains that, "every single word, line, sentence from the film is presented in the sketch along with abstract imagery that evokes the powerful and iconic place that is the Glass House."

This page: The Power of Place sketch is Esquer's response to *The Glass House Sketchbook* commission. It's one of 29 sketches made by various architects, designers, and artists inspired by the site.

Right and below: Pages from Esquer's personal sketchbooks.

DON'T KNOW

As well as pouring his creativity into books, Esquer gets a great deal from them. He reads everyday and says, "There are, and have always been incredible writers that with the power of pen, paper, and their imagination create worlds to share with you. Those worlds are inspiring, nourishing."

Esquer points to a quote from another source of inspiration. It comes from the Polish poet Wislawa Szymborska, who in her Nobel Lecture in 1996 said, "...Inspiration is not the exclusive privilege of poets or artists. There is, there has been, there will always be a certain group of people whom inspiration visits. It's made up of all of those who've consciously chosen their calling and do their job with love and imagination. It may include doctors, teachers, gardeners...I could list a hundred more professions. Their work becomes one continuous adventure as long as they manage to keep discovering new challenges in it. Difficulties and setbacks never quell their curiosity. A swarm of new questions emerges from every problem that they solve. Whatever inspiration is, it's born from a continuous 'I don't know'..."

Being led on a literary or poetic journey into a world created by an author is quite different to following an idea of your own when you don't know where it's going. The author's book has an ending, and we have a good sense of how far away that ending is because we hold it in our hands. Embarking on an open-ended journey, a continuous adventure of "I don't know" is courageous.

Adventurers don't go on expeditions without proper equipment though. The sketchbook can provide a retrospective trail for the journey and a place to rest. By recording how our ideas and our ability to develop them have grown we stay connected to the places we don't live anymore, the homelands of our inspiration.

This page: Esquer uses his sketchbooks as repositories for thoughts and ideas. He turns to them each day "for inspiration and creative energy."

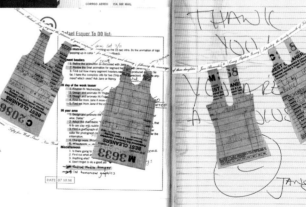

WHY NOT TRY...

Discovering your own form of sketchbook. Those people "who've consciously chosen their calling and do their job with love and imagination" and therefore receive a visit from inspiration had better have a place for it to sit. Having a sketchbook is like having a spare room or some extra shelves, somewhere to put things down instead of carrying them around, a way to keep our creative antenna free of clutter. A loving and imaginative way to be a designer is to keep a sketchbook. And a "sketchbook" can take absolutely any form you like.

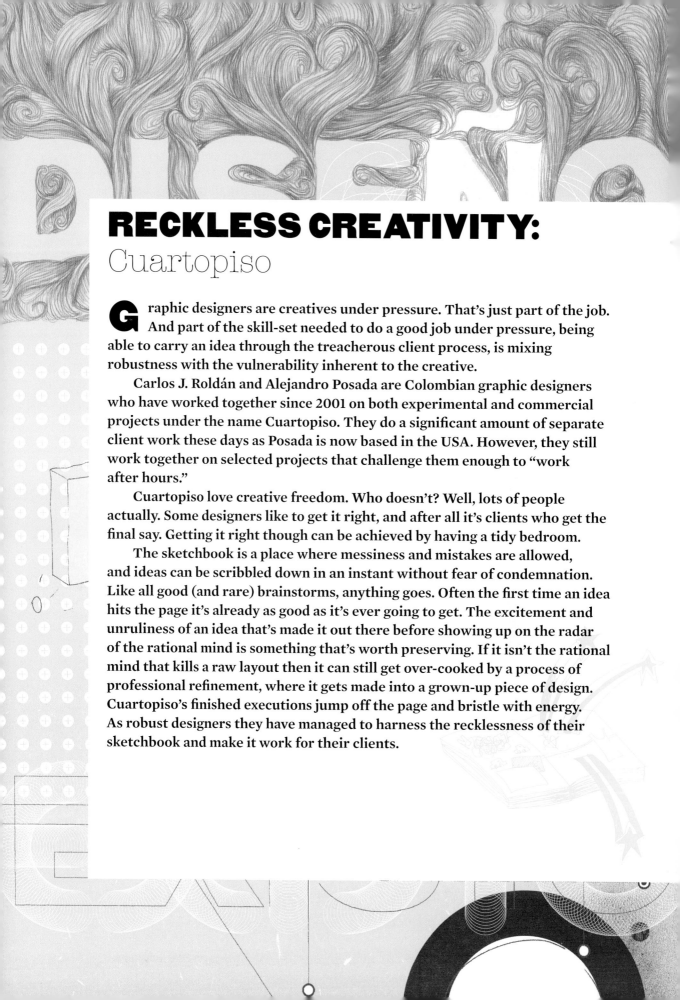

RECKLESS CREATIVITY:
Cuartopiso

Graphic designers are creatives under pressure. That's just part of the job. And part of the skill-set needed to do a good job under pressure, being able to carry an idea through the treacherous client process, is mixing robustness with the vulnerability inherent to the creative.

Carlos J. Roldán and Alejandro Posada are Colombian graphic designers who have worked together since 2001 on both experimental and commercial projects under the name Cuartopiso. They do a significant amount of separate client work these days as Posada is now based in the USA. However, they still work together on selected projects that challenge them enough to "work after hours."

Cuartopiso love creative freedom. Who doesn't? Well, lots of people actually. Some designers like to get it right, and after all it's clients who get the final say. Getting it right though can be achieved by having a tidy bedroom.

The sketchbook is a place where messiness and mistakes are allowed, and ideas can be scribbled down in an instant without fear of condemnation. Like all good (and rare) brainstorms, anything goes. Often the first time an idea hits the page it's already as good as it's ever going to get. The excitement and unruliness of an idea that's made it out there before showing up on the radar of the rational mind is something that's worth preserving. If it isn't the rational mind that kills a raw layout then it can still get over-cooked by a process of professional refinement, where it gets made into a grown-up piece of design. Cuartopiso's finished executions jump off the page and bristle with energy. As robust designers they have managed to harness the recklessness of their sketchbook and make it work for their clients.

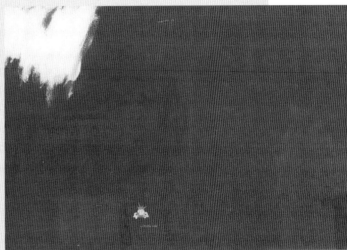

Top (left and right) and above:
Images from Cuartopiso's contribution
to The Place Project, in which, over 18
months, 35 designers from around the
world were asked to reflect on how
place influences creativity.
Left: Poster for *IdN* magazine
imagining graphic design 15 years
from now.

Top left: Poster from a conference about Cuartopiso's work.
Top right: Poster for the Philosophy Conference Cycle.
Right: Page from the OFFF Barcelona 2007 catalog.

WHY NOT TRY...

Being open about what your original ideas are and how exactly you'd like to see them manifested in the world. The raw creative act of making something out of nothing is captivating and most clients are excited by having access to more of the creative process than just the finished solution.

THE ART OF IMPROVISATION:

MasonBaronet

There is a myth—and being a myth doesn't make it any less true—that inspiration is a kind of spontaneous invention, a spark, a eureka. But another way of thinking of inspiration is as a flash mob of the mind: a mix of instructions, interpretations, and improvisations that generates a moment. Musicians call this method of working with the planned and the unplanned, the rehearsed and the improvised, a jam. The jamming session, far from being a pure moment of creative nirvana, depends on a repertoire of skills, the ability to conceptualize, and the art of interpretation.

Once a month, MasonBaronet, a full-service marketing communications firm based in Dallas, hold what they call Creative Jams. Scott Moore, an Art Director at MasonBaronet, explains their origins: "The Creative Jams have been going on for years. One of our original founders, Willie Baronet, established them as an unrestrained, freeform creative exercise. A way to freely flex your creative muscles, with as few limitations or constraints as possible."

In an age when deadlines rule, the MasonBaronet Creative Jam is not just a technique for exploring creativity without limitations, but also a device for discovering creative time, time that isn't paid for by the client or governed by the client's deadline time. As Art Director Jason Puckett points out, there's "no budget, branding, or client expectations." Like a jam, it's open-ended.

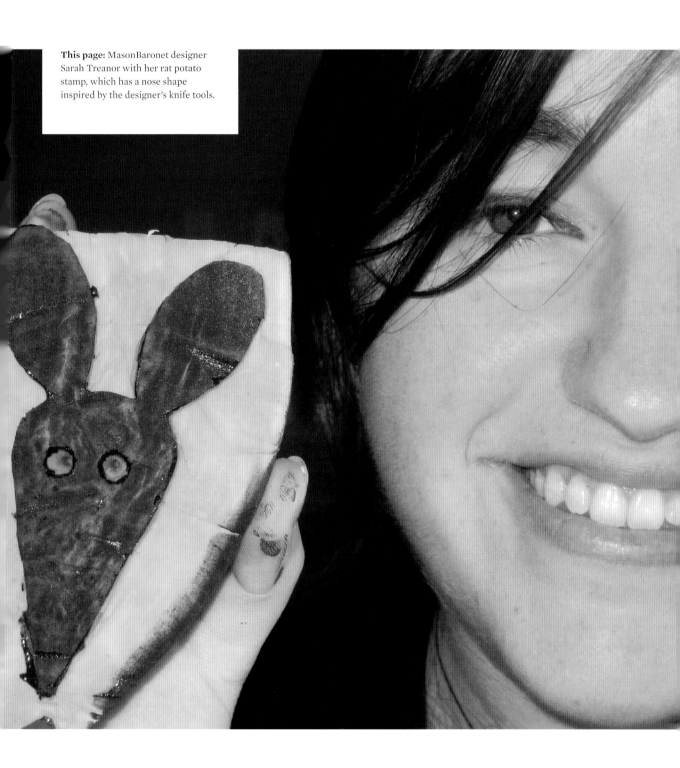

This page: MasonBaronet designer Sarah Treanor with her rat potato stamp, which has a nose shape inspired by the designer's knife tools.

POTATOES AND JAM

The Creative Jam usually takes place once a month and incorporates lunch, so the time devoted to it varies. "It could take 40 minutes to travel someplace and eat, leaving 20 minutes for the creative exercise," says Puckett. "Or we might take 10 minutes for lunch and use the rest of the time for creativity." A sense of place and environment is also an element of improvisation. It's not always the everyspace of the office. Though they are not explicit about this, it seems that the flexibility around the time devoted to making stuff, and where it happens, is actually part of the freed Jam mindset. "The host starts the Jam off by explaining the project and providing any necessary supplies (sketch paper, music, potatoes, etc.)," says Jason Moore. Though potatoes are not part of the Adobe Creative Suite, they have been used in Jams, prompted by a school project by the son of the creative director.

The Jam not only gives the creatives freedom from the external critical eye of the client, but it also frees them up internally by encouraging people not to be precious about ideas. It loosens up the internal critic who doesn't want to let go of things, or allow other ideas to emerge. And the format of the Jams also shapes a particular kind of thinking. "Since we only have an hour to create our project, the pace is fast, especially at the beginning. Lots of ideas are thrown around before we each settle on one. The Jams have helped hone my skills of developing simple and direct ideas," says Moore. It's interesting how being creatively time-sensitive, rather than client-time-sensitive, forces the creatives to be simple and direct. It's a great skill to learn. Puckett agrees, "although there really isn't time to be precious about your ideas in a Creative Jam. I usually stick with one of the first couple of ideas I have and make sure I take it through the course of the Jam. I am a list kind of a guy in these Jams, so I'll write down a few different things, pick one, and go with it."

STAYING WITH MISTAKES

Puckett talks through a recent Jam: "Everyone was asked the day before the Jam to write a story about a personal experience. Could be a paragraph, could be two pages. At the Jam, each person brought two copies of their story. With one copy, they had to go through it, sentence by sentence, and scratch out words that weren't necessary to the true message or subject of the story. In the end, they were to narrow it down to between two and five words; this became the title of their story. All titles had to start with 'The' plus their words in the order that they appeared in their story. Then they designed a logotype of their story title as it might be used on a movie poster. We had typeface books and Dover books with glyphs and letterforms for people to reference. At the end, each person read their story, shared their title, and showed their designs. There were some very personal and emotional stories shared in this one."

Because the Jams are improvised "on the road," so to speak, many of them are very hands-on, using materials and physical tools outside the familiar digital space. This has also had a direct impact beyond the Jam itself. The physicality of the process "is still a great place to start and a great way to generate ideas quickly," says Puckett. "It's harder to erase something than it is to click and delete, so sketches, mistakes, and experiments stay in front of you for a longer period of time. The hands-on approach and execution keeps me grounded in what design and creativity is all about and where it started. I take back the importance of being able to communicate an idea without worrying about kerning, stylistic photography, precision... if it doesn't work this way, it's not going to work in a computer layout."

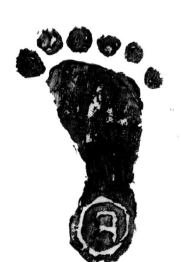

This spread: More stamps, including Scott Moore's six-toed foot, inspired by his 6ft 6in–frame.

APPLIED FREE ASSOCIATION

In musical terms, digital technology can lead to work that is underthought and overproduced, work that is overlaid with layer upon layer of tracks. The Creative Jam strips out, edits, takes away, gives the freedom and insight to subtract, which is the true art of improvisation. We always think of improvisation as an art of addition, but really it's the supremely difficult art of refining things, locking on to one aspect, spotting a pattern, and working it.

In the hectic day-to-day we often respond but we don't improvise. The rules and skills we learn can become armor for defending ourselves, rather than an imaginative palette to free associate with. The MasonBaronet Creative Jam is a form of applied free association in a space free from negative judgement. The Jam is a place not to play out an idea of perfect freedom and self-expression but to renew the knowledge and skills that have hardened and become encrusted over time. As David Sterrit writes in *Screening the Beats*, his book about jazz and beatnik culture, "Jazz historians provide many confirmations of the idea that previously learned material plays a central role in improvisation. Observing that improvisers must develop great familiarity with 'the (roughly) dozen chord types that most jazz improvising is based on,' James Lincoln Collier indicates that most jazz is rooted in a basic 'vocabulary' rather than an 'anything goes' boundlessness; he also describes the typical improviser's mind as being 'stuffed with a congeries of motifs, instrumental sounds, tiny figures, large structures, scales, chords, modes, and the rest of it,' from which the player 'works through association.'"

And sometimes this previously learned material goes back to the enthusiasm a child brings to the new skills they have learned. As Art Director Jason Moore says, "I'm still that five-year-old kid that loves to draw, paint, glue, and build. It's where I started as a little creative person, and where I still get most of my creativity today. The Jams remind me of that freedom."

Left: A visit to a local sculpture garden sparked a Jam where staffers pictured a fellow studio member. For Creative Director Paul Jerde, a piece of "multiarmed" sculpture seemed to capture the multitasking production manager Susan.

WHY NOT TRY...

Carving out an hour once a month, dedicated to an improvised creative project. Using intensely limited time restrictions can be a great way of training your "instinctive" creative focus, skilling yourself to create "on the fly." In any project research and planning is essential, but without improvisation, it is simply creative bureaucracy.

SIMPLE INSPIRATION:
Mark Gardner, Imaginary Forces

Designers get a limited amount of time to create and deliver a project. They need to be disciplined about their art to make sure they get things done within the window of time available, so a guiding principle or methodology that orientates them in an ongoing way makes getting going each time that bit smoother. There are many different ways of going about this and as many different ways of being a graphic designer. Some designers hone in on a style of image-making, whether consciously or unconsciously, so each client knows more or less what they will get by the delivery date, and that is the point. Clients shop for the "look" they want, and that's what they get. Other designers avoid working with a signature style, and instead are concerned with the appropriate communication of an idea.

Mark Gardner is a director at Imaginary Forces in New York. He directs live action as well as animation, doing a lot of graphic animation himself. He's also a talented stills photographer. His back catalog of moving image work includes commercials, short films, channel branding projects, and title sequences for movies, television shows, and events. He treats each client differently, arriving at an idea and an expression of that idea that fits the brief. Gardner peels away extraneous elements with the aim of leaving the intended communication unhindered. He says, "For me, it's important to continually be reducing down, clarifying, and distilling an idea until the function or concept of the piece and its form or style blend." Gardner admits he didn't always think like this, "at college and at times afterwards I was more than happy thinking a beautiful composition or a distinctive style was enough, or that a strong artistic idea was sufficient despite being crudely realized; but I rarely get satisfaction from one thing over the other anymore."

"Making the simple complicated is commonplace; making the complicated simple, awesomely simple, that's creativity."

Charles Mingus

Two of Gardner's projects have been inspired by, indirectly and directly, two giants of modernist design. "I think when art or design works it's when those two things [a distinctive style and a strong artistic idea] fuse, and no one did it better than Saul Bass and Paul Rand." He explains there "are many similarities between Rand and Bass. Both believed absolutely in the integrity of what they did. They believed that form and function were of equal importance, and that good design and creativity wasn't a matter of your taste vs. mine, but something quantifiable. If you communicated your idea then you were successful, if not you had failed."

Gardner collaborated with fellow Imaginary Forces director Steve Fuller to create the title sequence for *Mad Men*, a TV drama about advertising executives in 1960s' Madison Avenue. Authenticity and period detail were very important to the show's creator Matt Weiner, and this is reflected in the impeccable writing and art direction throughout the series. However, the period is viewed very much through a contemporary lens, and Gardner's brief was to capture these two elements in the title sequence.

In some ways Bass is an obvious design reference, having created so many iconic title sequences circa 1960, but the job wasn't

This page and following page:
Stills from the title sequence for the *Mad Men* TV show.

CASTING BY
BETH **BOWLING** &
KIM **MISCIA**

JOY THE BEST AMERICA HAS TO OFFER

PRODUCTION DESIGNER
BOB **SHAW**

EXECUTIVE PRODUCER MATTHEW **WEINER**

MAD MEN

simply to borrow a look that belonged to the era (a temptation many designers have given into) and a pastiche of a 1960s show would have undermined the intelligence of the series. Bass certainly had a "look" (flat colors, bold and simple graphic shapes, kinetic typography) that was partly defined by what could be technically achieved with film optics in the 1950s and 60s. Gardner says "it's often the discipline of these kinds of constrictions that produces the most creative work." Though the scenes from the *Mad Men* titles are rigged in 3D, Gardner and Fuller avoided the temptation to use more of the tricks that contemporary technologies make available. The sequence is edited as if it was a piece of live action, and the camera hardly moves except for one POV shot. Bass always had a good idea that showed through his stylish and raw executions. What he did so well for directors such as Hitchcock, Preminger, and Kubrick, was to summarize the psychological state of a

character, or of the movie itself, making a dreamlike mini-narrative that prepared the viewer for the first frame of the film and became an integral part of the storytelling process.

The *Mad Men* sequence needed to communicate the central theme of the show: a man both in control of and totally lost in a world he has created. The final image of the confident executive in his chair was the image that won Gardner and Fuller the job for Imaginary Forces, being, in Matt Weiner's eyes, a metaphor for the whole show. It was used on posters, promos, and mail-outs. There's something unsettling about seeing the man falling (to his death?) and then the next moment sitting down confidently in his office again. Impressionistic and simple rather than literal, the images set up jarring expectations that hang in the back of the mind while watching the show.

Though the sequence is filled with references to the 1960s advertising industry in New York, ultimately the look is contemporary. Gardner explains that, "the concept of the continual dreamlike fall throughout the sequence was actually inspired by a more contemporary Saul Bass sequence, for Martin Scorsese's *Casino*."

Paul Rand is another exemplar of simplicity in graphic communication. The One Club commissioned Gardner to produce a short film to be shown at their annual awards show where Paul Rand was to be

This page: Stills from a short film about Paul Rand, commissioned by and screened at The One Club.

posthumously inducted into The One Club Hall of Fame. Gardner explains, "Paul Rand notoriously thought very little of the moving image and the idea of having his work animated, accompanied by a recorded interview, would probably have had him rolling in his grave. Forever conscious of this I wanted to make something as simple as the work he produced with the same wit, irreverence, and sense of fun he showed to his clients throughout his career."

Like Bass and Rand, Gardner believes in the integrity of what he does. The work, rather than looking like a strictly recognizable set of executions, emerges from a guiding principal, almost a belief system, that graphic design is a useful and unique tool for communicating ideas in an awesomely simple way.

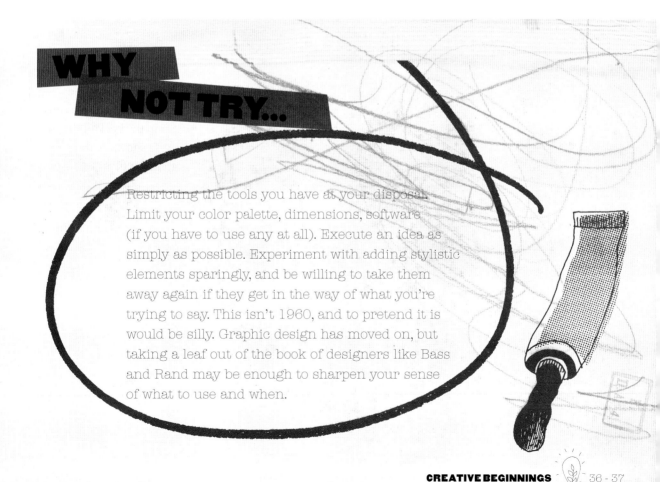

WHY NOT TRY...

Restricting the tools you have at your disposal. Limit your color palette, dimensions, software (if you have to use any at all). Execute an idea as simply as possible. Experiment with adding stylistic elements sparingly, and be willing to take them away again if they get in the way of what you're trying to say. This isn't 1960, and to pretend it is would be silly. Graphic design has moved on, but taking a leaf out of the book of designers like Bass and Rand may be enough to sharpen your sense of what to use and when.

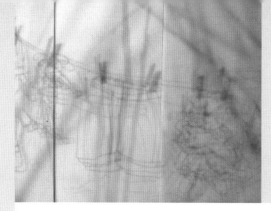

INSPIRATION AS STORYTELLING:
Joel Armstrong

We ask a lot of inspiration. But when you boil things down (always a good start when you are looking for inspiration), inspiration pulls together a whole bunch of material into creative focus. A lot of the time, especially in our professional projects, we look for inspiration in our research on the client, or wider research that's connected in a less direct way to the brief. But the most promising and sometimes challenging inspiration can be found in personal experience.

Inspiration gives shape to a whole bunch of information. It gives form, and when it comes to visual culture, finding a form is finding a visual language. And while a visual language is by definition something that is accessible to everyone, what goes with it is a new facility to talk with yourself in a different way. That's what makes it creative, it's a new vehicle of self-understanding, and understanding is the beginning of inspiration.

Joel Armstrong is a lecturer at John Brown University in Arkansas, where he has taught graphic design, drawing, and illustration. One of the many extraordinary things Armstrong has done is to fashion a visual language of illustration in wire. His inspiration gravitates around the dynamic of "loss" and reframing and reforming that loss with work that is about "discovery." It ranges from work that deals with the inevitable sense of loss (mixed with pride) you have with graduating students who you've nurtured, worked with, and learned from, to more serious and psychologically debilitating losses.

Right: Images from the show *One Body*.

OVER THE EDGE

Armstrong was originally trained in painting and drawing but got work as an art director for an oil production company. "I knew nothing about rubber cement or t-squares, and they thought someone who could draw well could obviously be an art director," he says. He developed his portfolio and got his breakthrough designing a poster for the Dallas Opera, that as he says "started off a career that lasted for quite a long time. For 20 years I flip-flopped between being an art director and an illustrator, and finally ended my 'graphic design' career as an art director for a publication, which lasted for nine and a half years in itself."

But then something happened which changed Armstrong's direction. "'The Lost Years' as I call them, pretty much put an end to my career as art director, illustrator, artist, graduate student, and teaching assistant. I was diagnosed in the late 1990s with bipolar disorder and the diagnosis plus medication

put me over the edge." He took medical leave from his job with the publisher, but the job wasn't there when he returned. "For months I didn't want to leave the house, get out of bed, or even take showers. I'm sure I was a blast to live with...but my family made it through those tough years," and on top of everything else he tried to get work but couldn't because his "legs and arms were constantly moving."

BENT OUT OF SHAPE

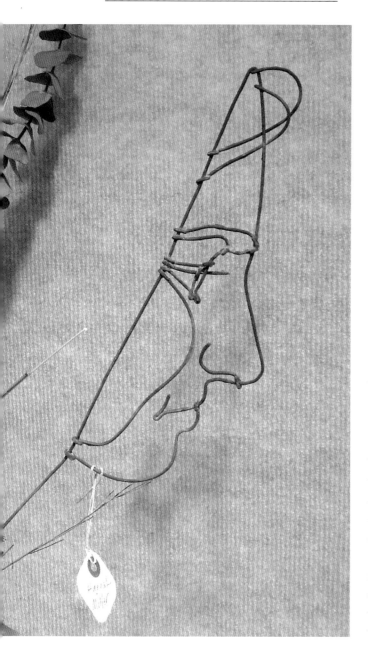

In that curious way in which creativity can find a way to transform unproductive material, Armstrong reimagined his illustration, and someone who was literally "bent out of shape," found a material that he could reform. "My only contentment," he says, "came from working with wire. I was able to work with [it] because it was a medium I could bend into shape. I was able to finish up my MFA during this time."

During his Master of Fine Arts Armstrong found himself having to prove "to the drawing faculty and myself that I could work beyond the boundaries of illustration. In my learning and experimentation, I got interested in Installation Art. In doing the installations, I found myself needing a personal vocabulary that could be used to help the overall reading by the audience. For various reasons, rust, clothing, and fish became my most readable elements. My thesis show was a visual demonstration of what it was to be bipolar. You look just fine, but inside you are scared to death." His show *Bipolar Disorder: Drawn and Quartered* "explained a lot in terms of my constant activity, workaholic tendency, and constant depression in the mix of good times."

Armstrong is also sustained by his religious faith, which generates an aesthetic of things being held together, being made whole. *One Body* was also the first work where he began to use found objects, things

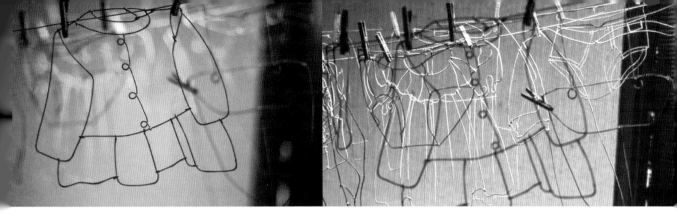

that had a certain aura. "*One Body* was the first time I took objects from others and used them as the sole basis of a show. I collected objects that meant something to the students and [using wire], created an image of *One Body*, the one body of Christ." It's a portrait of the student body. Another work, *Clothesline* is "a day's worth of laundry that first woke me up to the reality that my constant business meant I was missing my children growing up."

Left: Wire profile of a student from the *One Body* show.
Top left and right: Images from the *Clothesline* show.
Right: "This installation, *It's time to address'er drawers*, is based on letters that my Mom wrote, as a journal," says Armstrong. "She never mailed them, but kept them in the top drawer of her dresser. One of the letters spoke of verbal and physical abuse between my parents; I took all the words of the letter, and created them out of wire. The audience was able to take the words out of the dresser and give new life to them. This image is of the lamp, dresser, and drawer with the letters."

STORYTELLING

Armstrong's work may be conceptual, taking the form of installations occasionally, but at the heart of it is the illustrator's art of storytelling, and strictly speaking he's not so much occasionally inspired by "found" objects in his life as "found storytelling." Another of his projects—an installation called *Garage Sale*—will take a few years to

This page: *(Emersion) The Sign of Jonah*. In this piece, Armstrong tried to "capture the feeling of fishing, but from the underwater perspective."

complete and involves a very American institution. "Every Friday through Saturday, signs go up in intersections that point you to the location of someone's yard or garage sale. People put out their 'spring cleaning.' Things tend to become cheaper as the days go on, but if you wait til the end, what you want could be gone. I have been going to these garage sales with the understanding that I have $5 to spend. I explain to those in charge that I am looking for objects that were once of great value to them, and that are now in the garage sale. How did it lose favor? What is the story behind the piece?"

Armstrong tries to balance the demands of teaching with creating his own work. "It took a few rough years, and I am constantly trying to get my medication in order. Things are going quite smooth now. One of the major problems with the medication is it doesn't seem to allow sleep. Your mind goes so fast it won't relax. My creative energy has been steady, and to this day I try to produce a piece of art a day, large or small, just with the knowledge I can still create."

Thrown back on his own basic resources, Armstrong depends on his creative faculty. His inspiration is the daily rediscovery and exercise of the creative process, telling his story, and the heart of that story is that he creates. Sometimes it's easy to forget the internal resources we can call on; the will to create is sometimes enough to spark inspiration.

Using domestic objects for creative possibilities.
Working with objects from our personal space is
a reminder that we only loan out our creativity
to clients. They don't own it. It's our creativity as
human beings that enables us to be professional.
It is essential to explore our creative space—that's
not for sale.

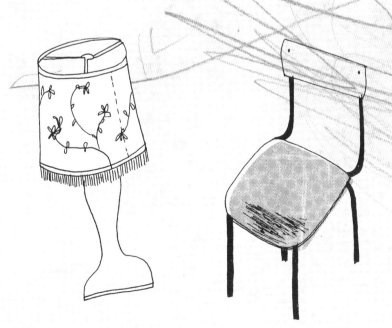

TWO:
Creative Rhythm

Whether it starts with a little spark or an explosion of fireworks, the beginning is a creative moment in time, a start point in a journey, but to where? What comes next? What is there to do when the fireworks start to fade and the honeymoon period is over?

The energy generated by a beginning is fragile and neglected ideas can fizzle out. The key is to make a beginning into part of an ongoing creative process, a continuum that carries an idea along, a life story rather than a flash in the pan. What follows the beginning? How do you handle the middle section? What is the best way to end? These questions apply to both the project itself and to the designer's life.

Each part of a creative life is significant. There's the obvious stuff, the time spent thinking about a project, time spent with a computer, camera, pencil, etc. Then there's downtime. How and when we stop, what we do when we stop—these things also contribute to how sharp a creative we are when we're working. Do you work better at 7am or 7pm? Do you need naps or bananas? A rest or a run? Do you need to soak up an exhibition or just look at the clouds drifting by? Finding a rhythm for all these ways of working, feeding, and resting, finding a way for them to hold together as a whole, is the most important creative challenge for anyone wanting to regularly make high-quality work.

CREATIVE FITNESS:
Noah Scalin

The professional designer's creativity is commodified by the client process, and is therefore also given a boundary. The idea starts here, and ends there. Something that is often referred to as "flowing" (when it works, at least) is turned into a quantifiable unit. More stop-start than flow. Clients can buy small ones and large ones, single units or several at once.

It's understandable, then, to be tricked into thinking that creativity is finite, and ideas, exhaustible. However, most people who have gone through the process of becoming physically fit through regular exercise know that the fitter a body becomes, the farther away the point of exhaustion lies.

ANOTHER LIMITED REBELLION

More exercise is rewarded by greater ability (there really is plenty more where that came from), but in a busy practice where the client's needs can seem all-consuming, the idea of having more exercise to do each day can be daunting. Nevertheless, on June 3, 2007, Noah Scalin, founder of Virginia-based Another Limited Rebellion, had the idea of making a skull, or a representation of one, every day for a whole year. Skull-A-Day was born, almost on a whim.

"It was a total lark!" Scalin explains. "The thought just crossed my mind one day and a couple days later I made my first skull and posted it online without thinking too much about what was really involved in committing myself to a year of creative work!" Even though some days that amounted to over four hours' work, the effort has paid off.

Personal creative work can get sidelined if there's no reason to finish it by a specific date. One of the great things about Scalin's project is that he has created an incredibly simple and structured brief: see a skull in a different way, 365 times. The challenge, every day, is to be open to the world, and have faith that it'll be there, somewhere, in a worn piece of plastic or (with a bit of prodding) in a pile of pencil shavings, or

Left: Skull 281, made from a kneaded eraser.
Below: Skull 283, made from 2,099 cotton swabs.

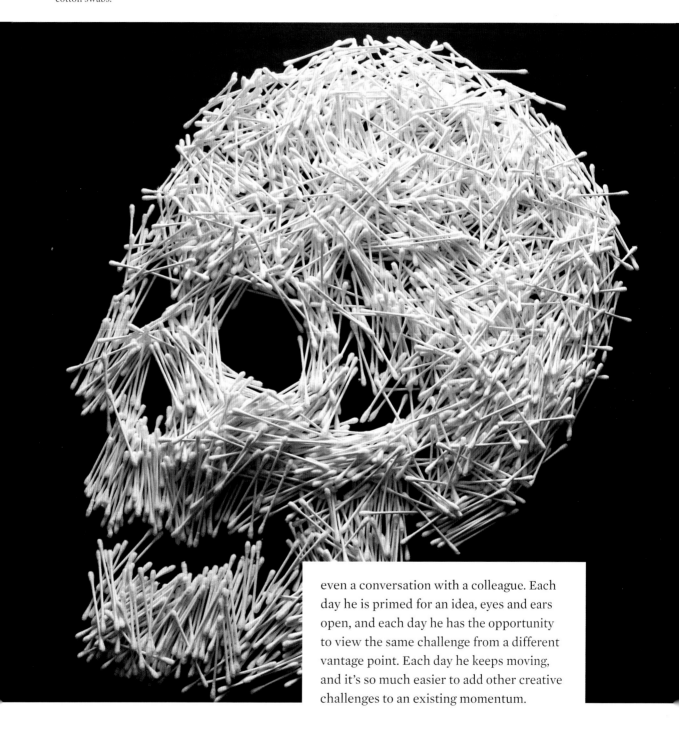

even a conversation with a colleague. Each day he is primed for an idea, eyes and ears open, and each day he has the opportunity to view the same challenge from a different vantage point. Each day he keeps moving, and it's so much easier to add other creative challenges to an existing momentum.

UNFAMILIAR TERRITORY

Scalin had used up all his regular responses after 100 days and found himself in less familiar territory, working with different tools, perceiving things in quite different ways, and having a fuller experience of his creative potential. "I had to be constantly aware of my surroundings and open to thinking about things in new ways. I would often see something in the morning that inspired me by the afternoon. It has given me an opportunity to explore a wide range of media and techniques that I normally wouldn't get to do. It also helped me improve my photography skills and hone my ability to create good work on short deadlines."

Scalin's creative prowess quickly grew, and thanks to the speedy distribution of the Skull-A-Day blog, the project also grew rapidly from a "total lark" to a personal project that was witnessed by thousands of people (many of whom were sufficiently inspired to send in their own skulls, which are featured alongside Scalin's on skulladay. blogspot.com) and then onto a book solely dedicated to Skull-A-Day.

The final skull was completed on June 2, 2008. While Scalin, fueled by the success of Skull-A-Day, prepares to move onto his next projects, the blog site will be kept running for at least six months, featuring a skull from a different reader each day.

This is a lot of growth from a "lark," an urge one day to set a creative challenge that could be fun. So, rather than exhaustion representing a wall, it can instead represent the need for a pause, a rest, before the next flow of creativity begins and ideas get a chance to go beyond what seemed possible in the beginning.

Left: Skull 287, made from fabric woven through a chainlink fence.
Middle: Skull 357, made from nude bodies.
Above: Skull 360, made from a carved cabbage.

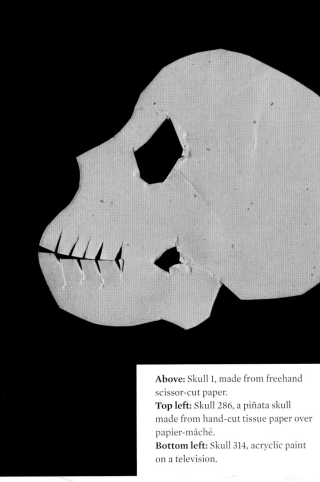

Above: Skull 1, made from freehand scissor-cut paper.
Top left: Skull 286, a piñata skull made from hand-cut tissue paper over papier-mâché.
Bottom left: Skull 314, acrylic paint on a television.

WHY NOT TRY...

Exercising so you can grow stronger. Do more in order to have more. If you don't already have a regular exercise, why not start one? Start small. Do something manageable that could take as little as five minutes on one of your more blisteringly hectic days. It could be so easy to set up something that's too demanding only to dump it on day three. If it works, allow it to grow. Skull-a-day is a particularly structured project. This may work for you, but alternatively less structure, or no structure at all may be exactly what could add something valuable right now.

Right: Front cover of *100 Days of Monsters*. The accompanying DVD includes video clips of the Monsters being created.

ONGOING PROJECTS:
Stefan G. Bucher, 344 Design

"The Daily Monsters came out of a need to do something spontaneous and happy," says Stefan G. Bucher, a Los Angeles-based graphic designer working for a variety of clients in the music and publishing industries, among others. "A lot of my work is very detail-printed and time-intensive, so the monsters provided an antidote."

The Daily Monster is a good example of a regular creative exercise. Every day Bucher films himself creating a drawn monster. He drops some black ink onto a white piece of paper and blows the ink across the page using a straw. He's left with a random splurge of ink that he spontaneously responds to by adding considered drawn lines and (sometimes) color to create an intricate Monster. The process is filmed and truncated by a time-lapse process before being posted online. At that point readers are invited to write the story of the Monster, bringing it to life in their own way and giving it a dimension outside of Bucher. The project has grown enormously. There are well over 200 days of monsters and stories, the first 100 of which have been compiled into a book and a DVD.

It's always a privilege to watch an artist at work, and it's fascinating to watch the Monster films and witness Bucher's spontaneity in process. It's not surprising that Bucher has created a strong audience with these films, along with his invitations to participate and collaborate.

Below: Spreads from *100 Days of Monsters.*

Above: A Monster mural in Nebraska.
Right: The Monster-making process.

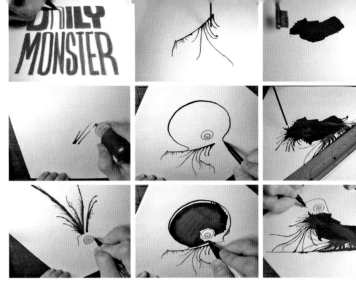

Bucher's enthusiasm and openness are clearly contagious. He has attracted an audience that has become his studio colleague and his foil. The monsters provided an "antidote" to the tyranny of detailed client work and the scarily long hours that designers often work in order to get projects finished to a high level. Rather than having a moan and a groan to a friend after a long day at work, Bucher has found a way to let off steam constructively. His audience responds to his inky grumbles and they share the burden by inventing a life for them and taking them somewhere else.

WHY NOT TRY...

Doing something each day that is different to the rest of the work you do. Break out from the parts of yourself you usually use, and use or develop an opposite skill. One-armed press-ups are deeply impressive and no doubt a sign of great strength, but doing them on a daily basis, exclusively with the right or the left arm, would lead to a (monstrous?) physical form that wouldn't function very well as a whole. Which creative muscle could you benefit from resting while you pump another one instead?

FLOW:
Robin Rimbaud aka Scanner

Creativity doesn't come in a packet, even though it often ends up in one. Ideas don't pop out fully formed. They don't have an edge, and there's no clear beginning or end. Glimpsing into the unpackaged world of creativity and finding an idea is a very private affair. Active creatives respond to ideas they've found by molding them into a shape that means they can be shared in some way. This shaping is the process of *working* creatively, and without this work ideas would remain silent, invisible, and unformed. Left to its own devices creativity could just go on and on, ebbing and flowing, at no point becoming any *thing*. For professionals there's usually the help of a brief or a commission, some kind of temporal expectation that focuses the creative worker, spurring them firstly into action and then on to a conclusion.

Robin Rimbaud, aka Scanner, is a British artist who is consciously engaged in the tension between stopping and starting, between being free and being limited. He says, "I find that I respond to restrictions, deadlines, schedules. I'm at my weakest when given an opportunity to work with no fixed timeline, for example a new record for a label, a possible film collaboration, etc."

Scanner's main passion is music, though he has varied interests and likes to mix things up. At the top of his online biography it states that he's an artist who "traverses the experimental terrain between sound, space, image, and form." He has performed, created, and installed works in many of the world's most prestigious exhibition spaces, and collaborated with many high-profile artists from an array of disciplines, including musicians and composers, filmmakers and video artists, dancers and choreographers. He has released several recordings of his experimental compositions, and sound-designed a feature film, as well as a car horn!

Scanner has worked hard and achieved world renown for his intensive creative output. He doesn't like stopping for long. "I work from the flow of one production to another, usually at any one point focusing on at least six to 12 different projects." He goes on, "There hasn't been a moment [since 1990] when I've paused for more than two

Below: Live performance at the
Holland Festival 2005.
Bottom: Breakthrough Recording
Installation at the *WAVES* exhibition
in the Arsenals exhibition hall of the
Latvian National Museum of Art in
Riga, 2006. Sound work using
recordings made in spaces with
ghostly associations.

weeks without creating new work, or
recycling work, interpreting, mixing,
exploring new avenues and channels."

He has a varied existence, working on
multiple projects simultaneously, as he
"traverses" both geographical borders and
boundaries in art and design. It sounds like
it could be a giddy experience, however he
has his anchor: "I work to a fairly strict
schedule which I rarely move from. I wake
up early. I begin work almost immediately,
then work all day until around 19.00 at the
latest. I very rarely ever work in the
evenings and never at night."

Below: Turning Light, Walkergate
Park Hospital, Newcastle upon Tyne,
UK. A permanent light and sound
installation in the swimming pool of a
new hospital specializing in services
for people with neurological and
neuropsychiatric conditions.

ORDINARY CREATIVITY

Creativity has historically been presented as an esoteric activity; a mysterious gift bestowed upon a precious few. And even though the increasing democratization of creativity has blurred the division between people who are creative and those who are not, creativity is still referred to as a curious phenomenon. Not for Scanner though, "I'm just a simple, disciplined person, rather restlessly exploring all channels of creativity to see what's possible. My habits are banal, nothing extraordinary at all. I must confess

to finding nothing intrinsically mysterious about the idea of creativity, it's just something that flows from my body and mind."

This goes against the cliché of the artist who must sweat blood in the realization of the work. The cliché supports the idea of the creative act as something incredibly precious, and that ideas must be teased out of the ether and labored over for a long time by the talented artist in order to secure the highest quality.

For Scanner, brevity is crucial, "The key aspect for me is to always complete the work as soon as possible, to meet the deadline immediately, rather than let work develop over a time. The faster I seem to produce a work the more successful and rewarding it is."

From left to right, top to bottom:
Cover feature for *The Wire* music journal, with photos by Tim Kent, 1999.
Feature for *The Wire* with photos by Tim Kent, 1999.
52 Spaces live show, 2003. 52 Spaces used sounds of the city of Rome and elements of Antonioni's *L'eclisse* (1962) to create the soundtrack for an image of a city suspended in time, anonymous and surreal.
The Nature of Being live cinema performance with Olga Minkat at the Mapping Festival, Geneva, 2008.
Live performance at the Miskin Theatre, UK, 2006.
Live performance in Barcelona as part of the Störung Festival, 2007.

IMPROVISATION

Much of Scanner's prolific output is experiential and improvised. He is well known for his earlier work that controversially involved intercepting (scanning) the mobile telephone conversations of unsuspecting individuals and using them as raw material for his compositions, particularly in his live performances. Scanner says of the live improvised work, "having no anticipation where the conversation would turn next, what would be revealed next, the sudden changes in a flash, have clearly reflected upon my work these days too, in that they are never finished. The performances are of that moment, not to be repeated—that's very important to my work."

For Scanner the process of creating is as ordinary as anything else he could be doing. Antenna extended and switched on ready to scan the world, his creativity simply "flows" from his body and mind; something he clearly relishes in his live performances when his "flow" is shared by his audience in a "not to be repeated" performance. Stopping at 19.00 everyday gives his time a neat rhythm of stopping and starting, a regular beat around which he can hang whatever he likes and that makes the broader experience of his life into a constant flow of creative output.

Top: Live performance in Tokyo 2002 with D-Fuse motion graphic artists. **Above:** 3 bis F Gallery, part of the Arborescence Festival in Aix-en-Provence, France, 2006. This installation explored the idea of landscape and the resonance and meaning of the surroundings in relation to Cezanne and the Provence countryside. The exhibition consisted of 12 large-scale digital prints, a floor sculpture created from 300 bottles, a wall drawing of apples contributed by the public in exchange for a free apple, and an isolation cell where sounds and smells were used to suggest images of the mountains.

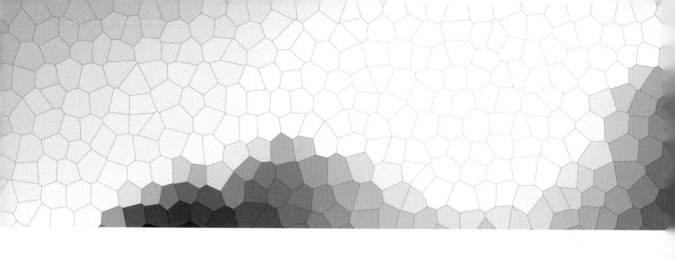

External structures like deadlines are simultaneously dreadful and crucial. To a creative in mid-flow, an ending can look like an aggressive ultimatum, but a deadline gives impetus to the manifestation of the creative flow, in the absence of which some of the most brilliantly formed ideas in the world would have instead just trickled away. There are no real endings creatively in that ideas can be revisited and developed. Looking for an idea is an ordinary process, but it's still easy to get lost unless there's something to return to. Somewhere along the line there has to be a pause, and a place to rest. Knowing how to stop is a crucial part of being able to start.

Top and below: Installation at the Arborescence Festival.
Middle: Liverpool Life public billboard project, 2005. This project focused on the concept of life imprisonment and the fact that it means different things in different countries.

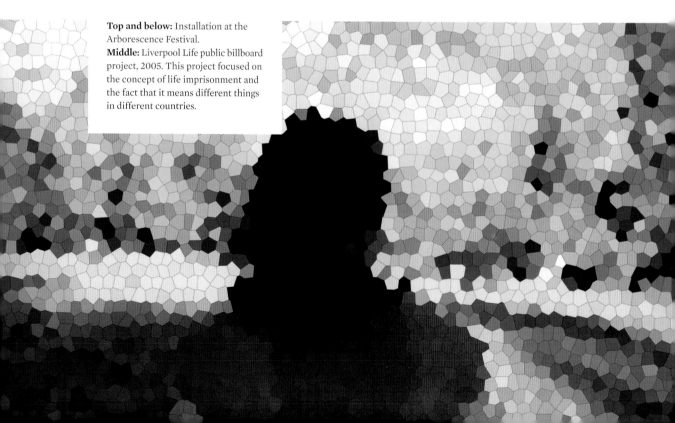

WHY NOT TRY...

Different methods of stopping with the aim that starting up again will be easier. It takes less effort to keep something moving than it does to get it started from scratch each time. The novelist Haruki Murakami has talked about stopping work each day at a point where he could write more. He doesn't completely finish because by doing so he would interrupt the flow and have to start up again afresh. Leaving loose threads exposed means there's always something tangible to grab hold of when you return to work.

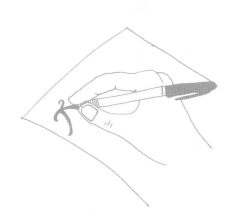

HANDMADE TRADITION:
Studio AND

For many creatives, whether you are a guitarist, an acrobat, a chef, or a designer, at some point in your act of imagination, it all comes down to trust in your hands. For over 10 years Jean-Benoit Levy of Studio AND collected images of hand signage from all over the world. The images were eventually compiled and processed by various people at the studio to create a font, H-AND-S. As Levy explains, "We passed the project from intern to intern, and it grew until I hired one ex-intern to clean up those almost 200 hand signs using Illustrator. Two other interns worked on the implementation on Fontographer. After an undefined amount of hours and almost 10 years of growing, a font was born."

This page: Street poster for the Hand Museum in Lausanne, Switzerland.

TRÈS TOUCHER / TOUCHE-ATOUT

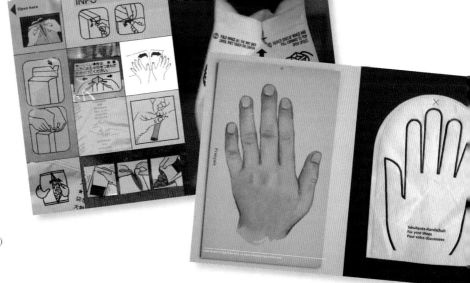

Right: Spreads from *Handbook*, a book of hand images, exploring the visual language of "signs and codes, symbols and icons, motion and gestures, interpretations and styles."
Below left: Figure for the US keyboard, showing: "normal" (above) and "shift" (below).
Below right: Examples from the H-AND-S font.

Passing this project from hand to hand, the designers built a visual language from product information icons—icons that show us how to act, to pour, to open, to make. They are modern hieroglyphs that Levy has abstracted from basic icons. It's a fascinating piece of applied visual sociology. In *Handbook*, a book that arose out of the collection, Levy writes, "Hand signs can express complexity as they can improve simplicity in our daily life. Crossing over the multiple barriers formed by the countless national languages, the use of these modern hieroglyphs remains as effective for communicating now as it was prior to the development of speech."

Levy and the studio have developed a universal language of "gestures," a formalized graphic of self-expression. The symbol of the hand is both deeply personal and also universal. It's no accident that this project became its own journey of inspiration. The project was literally handed down from colleague to colleague, as a new tradition, inspiration forming a bond from designer to designer. Sometimes inspiration takes time, it can't be hurried, it needs to be handmade.

GESTURES AND INSTRUCTIONS

H-AND-S FULL
Figures for Us keyboard, above: "normal" / below: "shift"   Copyright: 1996–2006 / www.and.ch

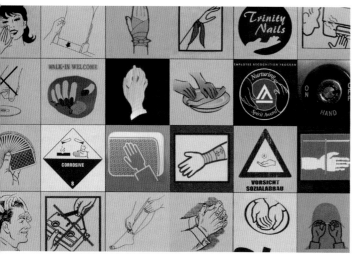

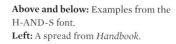

Above and below: Examples from the
H-AND-S font.
Left: A spread from *Handbook*.

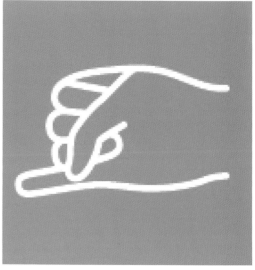

WHY NOT TRY...

Creating a project that establishes your own tradition within your studio. Normally we commercialize "tradition" as a portfolio or a showcase of client work. Tradition is where you can locate and explore creative values and identity as opposed to showcasing creative skill. In our world where we are called on to constantly call out the "new," a project that houses and creates tradition is a priceless creative touchstone.

...lic Hints.

...and everything in its place

...as, do not spend more than 1d/11¼

...life again, nicrorea...
will be occasioned...
fine sand to kill birds will... ...or b...
when so desired by naturalists, or for o...

CONVERSATION...

221. *Potato-Snow, a favourite way of cooking Potatoes.*—
Choose white, mealy, smooth potatoes; skin them; boil them
carefully, and when they crack pour off the water, and put them
to dry on the trivet till quite dry and powdery. Rub them
through a coarse wire-sieve on the dish they are to go to table
on; and do not move it or the flakes will fall and flatten.

THREE:
Collecting Inspiration

It might be an image in the corner of a magazine, a piece of writing in a journal, a tune that always delivers us to some inspirational place, or a discarded photograph we find on the floor. Imagination can be fired at any point by the things we come into contact with. By collecting together these pointers and keeping them with us, in a book or on the wall in front of us, we prolong that contact and thereby take ownership of it.

Collections are reminders, friends, evidence of a life. We turn ourselves inside out when we fill a room or a book with our collections. Like good friends, the books, the music, and the imagery we turn to for inspiration share and reveal things we thought we already knew. It's why we need to keep our collections fresh.

Collecting inspiration is a kind of dreaming, pulling together fragments, images, and ideas so we can explore a story they are trying to tell us. It's why so much great art is based on these fragments of inspiration, seeing how they fit together, from montage to cut-ups.

Collecting inspiration is about building an archive of secret knowledge, drawing together a collection of prophetic objects that only makes sense afterward. We need to think of collections as our little theater of objects. Let them play out a story and see what happens.

COLLECTIONS:
Lizzie Ridout

It's every creative's most seductive and most compelling desire—the desire to begin at the beginning. To put it another way, how many times have you put off starting something, because you don't know where to start? Designers often talk about the difficulty of making that first "mark." There's always a desperate temptation not to begin until an idea is fully formed, but it can never be formed at all until you put it down on paper, and one mark doesn't make much sense until you commit to the second mark, which is when it really begins to mean something. Lots of things happen, and many possibilities emerge, in the gap between the first mark and the second mark; and as the French psychoanalyst Jacques Lacan mysteriously argued, it's that gap which is the beginning!

EIGHTY THOUSAND YEARS

Designer Lizzie Ridout got a position as the Pearson Creative Research Fellow at the British Library in London. The British Library collects everything, and it boasts that "if you see five items each day, it would take you 80,000 years to see the whole of the collection." Where to begin?

Ridout began a project about domestic objects, basing the idea on earlier work from her time at the Royal College of Art. "One project was a portrait in a public space and I started thinking about representing yourself through the possessions you own, and a lot of work began to be created from that."

At the British Library, Ridout worked with the idea that there was no obvious place to start, no natural beginning, steering clear of anyone with a body of knowledge who could have shaped a path for her. "I didn't want to work with curators. I was keen to be quite haphazard and not necessarily look for anything too specific. Keeping that general idea, I started looking at domestic objects that might have strange stories attached to them or were actually quite bizarre. I started in the paintings collection. It was quite random. I just gathered a massive amount of material."

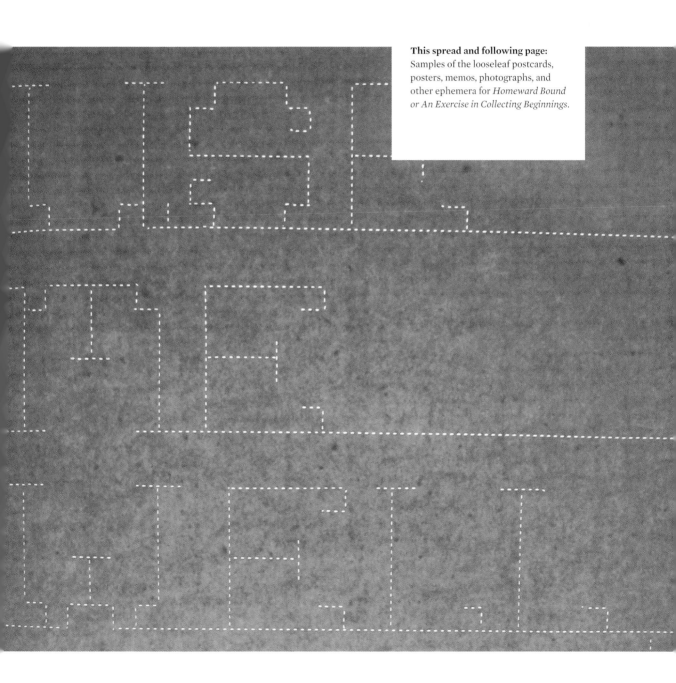

This spread and following page:
Samples of the looseleaf postcards, posters, memos, photographs, and other ephemera for *Homeward Bound or An Exercise in Collecting Beginnings*.

REVIVING A SHOT SPARROW

The result was Homeward Bound or An Exercise in Collecting Beginnings, an A4 (Letter)-sized folder holding sheets of curiosities and visual knick-knacks in all shapes and sizes, like an image of *Pattens, or walk-on-water shoes*; an image of Charlotte and Branwell Bronte's *Blackwoods Young Men's Magazine* from 1829; drawings of elf locks; and advice on how *To Revive a Shot Sparrow*. It is a treasure chest of arcane documents made significant by the fact that they were chosen. How you read them and understand their meaning, and the meaning of the piece as a whole, depends on which items you choose to look at first. Each element is a different point of departure. You assemble it differently each time. There is a bigger story being told and a mystery unfolding.

"Each piece informs the others in a different way," says Ridout. "That's what happens when you have one person looking for things, and that's why I didn't want to work with a curator or have other people looking for things for me." Beginnings demand a creative to make sense of what

exactly the beginning is, the point at which a creative process begins to make sense. It's why "design by committee" never works, because everyone sees different beginnings. "If there is an overriding theme," continues Ridout, "it sounds a bit macabre, but it's the idea of death. We are all heading to a particular destination, acquiring all this stuff, and yet it is all so pointless. That's why the Victorian theme ended up featuring so heavily. There is a parallel you can draw between the project I was doing and the way the Victorians thought—they were over-sentimental about everything, about belongings, about people."

Ridout's concluding thoughts lock onto another recognizable feature of the creative process. As much as beginnings are incredibly useful and valuable, we must always leave them behind. Don't get too attached to beginnings; don't get sucked into nostalgia for your beginning. You can always make a new one. Remember, the beginning only makes sense at the end.

WHY NOT TRY...

Listing out five radically different starting points for a project. Don't be precious about the beginning—your creative eye transforms it into something recognisably "project-like" very quickly.

FIND AND SEARCH:
Sophie Beard

The act of being creative is always about searching and finding at some level. Designers either have an idea or they search for one. Interesting designers are good at finding (or suddenly having) ideas, and the successful ones learn what to do with a good idea once they've gotten hold of one.

For Sophie Beard finding things is "a constant delight." She says of her practice, "all my work is about a collection or documentation of an observation of some kind. Put really simply, it's about my desire to show other people interesting things I have found." Beard trained as a graphic designer at the Royal College of Art (RCA) in London. She is currently working through a practice-based PhD examining the use of family photographs in newspapers, and she is a Senior Lecturer in Graphic Design at the University for the Creative Arts at Epsom. She isn't a regular graphic designer though. She doesn't have clients. "I see myself as a graphic designer. I am interested in 'Graphic Design Authorship,' in working without a client, and what this means for me is being involved in collaborative and self-initiated projects. What motivates me is the creative process of communicating particular and specific ideas."

"Graphic Design Authorship" is an interesting term that has gained in popularity over recent years. Traditionally the graphic designer has been the communicator of someone else's idea; a stealth worker who facilitates their client's message; a ghost typographer, photographer, animator, idea-generator, etc. Creatives who are authors of their own work could call themselves Artists, however the relationship between art and design is sketchier than it used to be and there's less need to be one or the other. Many artists of course have used graphic communication as their mode of expression and while the benefit of reclassifying artists who have employed these tools is highly debatable, designers gaining a framework for being authors of their own messages is a welcome development.

BIG BEN, LONDON.

Authorship itself is an ambiguous term, however in Beard's case it's simple: she claims authority over what she observes and the way she presents it, utilizing graphic skills of communication rather than anything else she is at liberty to use.

This page: A selection of Big Ben postcards.

The Clock Tower of The Palace of Westminster, or "Big Ben" as it is affectionately known (which is actually the nickname of the main bell inside the tower), was built in 1858 and is one of the most famous and photographed clocks in the world. Beard's project Counting Big Ben grew out of another project she started while at the RCA, about documenting time, however she didn't start collecting the postcards until a few years after that. It was in 2006 that she decided to start the collection and it is still ongoing. The collection tells the story of the Big Ben postcards by showing them, not in a chronological order historically, but instead by sequencing them according to the time of day they happen to display. "I like to impose rules and systems to the process of collecting." Beard says. "The limitations I impose help me creatively." The system

Big Ben

Big Ben

London

reveals a different kind of chronology, a secret history of the clock tower that is still emerging.

In The Readers Before Us, a project Beard made in collaboration with Allyson Waller while at the RCA, she scoured the college library for things that had been left in the books during their time out on loan. Personal notes, phone numbers, receipts, and doodles were among the variety of things that had been silently waiting between the pages of the books. Many of us have found something in a book before that didn't belong to us, and possibly thought little of it, but collectively these items reveal a previously hidden, subtle level of experience; things unearthed only by the process of searching for and documenting them.

"I am really interested in ephemera and finding intriguing objects that start to tell a story when part of a collection. The 'archive' element is very engaging as it is the constant search—the 'find'—that is most compelling." Beard finds something and then begins her real search. Her "constant delight" in finding things and her desire to show us what she's found is a perpetual inspiration.

The word "idea" is derived from the Greek word "idein" which means "to see." We all see in a unique way, that is a fact. The most illuminating thing Beard shows us is that there are many different layers of reality, all of which can be observed and in turn made visible. To see an idea, sometimes we need do nothing more than open our eyes and look with a sense of authority at what we find.

This page: More examples from Sophie Beard's collection of Big Ben postcards.

WHY NOT TRY...

Imposing strict rules on yourself and your project that support you in your process. Steven Sondheim said, "If you told me to write a love song tonight, I'd have a lot of trouble. But if you tell me to write a love song about a girl with a red dress who goes into a bar and is on her fifth martini and is falling off her chair, that's a lot easier, and it makes me free to say anything I want."

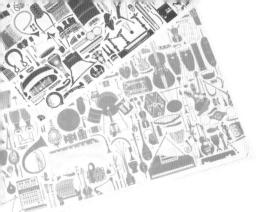

MAKING SENSE OF THINGS:
MWM Creative

Devotees and masters of color, geometric shape, and text, graphic designers love to order and clarify things. They analyze, categorize, make sense of, and ultimately represent the world in a way no other professional can.

Maria da Gandra and Maaike van Neck are MWM Creative. They are the designers and authors of *World Musical Instruments*, an extensive pictorial dictionary of musical instruments from around the world (the project is a development of da Gandra's MA project. Her thesis on western European musical instruments was expanded, after many conversations with the publisher, to include the rest of the world).

The book is a fastidiously constructed document, containing drawings of over 1,500 instruments presented at a consistent scale of 1:16.3. Notably, the drawings are arranged along a chronological timeline—though other criteria including geographical origin, type, musical pitch, and build material were also considered. Music, though, is a time-based medium, and arranging them in historical sequence, creating a straight line from the first to the last, gives readers the unique opportunity to picture the evolution of musical instruments.

Left: A work-in-progress spread.
Above left: Poster for *World Musical Instruments*.
Above right: Inspirational objects that formed part of the extensive research process.

MEMORY AND EXPERIENCE

Music is the most enigmatic of artforms. It is a powerful stimulant to our emotions and memories and yet it remains strangely intangible. We live in such a predominantly visual culture that even though more music is listened to now, both live and recorded, than at any time in history, it still takes second place to the power of the image. A personal music collection is as much a collection of sleeves as a collection of sounds. We listen to music one track, one beat, or one symphony at a time, but an entire collection can be visually scanned on an MP3 player in seconds. These visual representations are mnemonics for what the transient artworks mean to us, packaging experiences rather than things.

Musical instruments, however are exactly that—things. They are conduits for musicians who express their art by mastering their instruments. As MWM explain, "Not only do they make sound and music tangible, a musical instrument communicates its cultural surroundings, its heritage, and how they function on their own as well as in relation to other instruments."

WORLD OF INFORMATION

At the outset there was a mountain of information to process. Embarking on the book, MWM found that the "material was in many different formats and media; from books to journals to curators to museum collections to individual instrument makers to instruments found by chance—suddenly anything and everything making a sound was extremely important."

MWM have produced intricate pictograms for the book that retain detailed information about the instruments, only really omitting the material from which they are made. The selection of musical instruments isn't exhaustive, so they had to go through an initial editing process: "We never set out to document all musical instruments of the world (this is virtually impossible) and feel the selection of instruments works as an efficient representation." However, their ambition was greater than what ultimately proved possible within the constraints of the project. "If we had more time, money, etc., [the project] would have most likely resulted in a larger book."

The small studio where the project came together was filled with photocopies, scribbles, and books of various kinds. The process of boiling down a world of information into one comprehensive object was a formidable task, and took 10 months of seven-day weeks and 14-hour days. "The project asked for a great amount of discipline, time management, and organization due to the tight deadlines of university research funding and the huge amount of information to verify, order, and draw. The making of the book was a great exercise of theoretical and visual research.

"Resources such as books, periodicals, and other printed matter were not only important because of their historic value and opportunities to verify information, but as objects they also became a reminder. We still have most of the books in our office and this reminds us of the period of time working on the book."

During those long days and months organizing the book, this studioscape built from "reminders" of the end goal must have been heartening. Books are our collective memories. They function as milestones in history, legacies that are passed down through generations. Hermann Hesse wrote, "Without words, without writing, and without books there would be no history, there could be no concept of humanity." We may now need to add "pictograms" to Hesse's statement.

World Musical Instruments is a monumental mnemonic, densely packed with a history of humanity. The book feels special and it's difficult not to appreciate the incredible feat of organization that it represents. MWM have created an elegantly condensed ensemble of drawings; a distillation of a wealth of valuable information that otherwise would be simply too much to remember.

Below: Cover and spread from *World Musical Instruments*.

WHY NOT TRY...

Researching, ordering, and designing a record of something that personally interests you. You may or may not have taken advantage of assignments given to you by outside bodies like schools and universities. However you did it before, doing it for yourself could be a whole different story.

CURATING CHANCE:
Nick Clark

I'm not absolutely sure what my collection of junk or curiosities—as I prefer to think of them—has got to do with all this," says Nick Clark of the photograph shown on the right. The image shows his collection of objects above some of the professional work this stuff has inspired, and the reason it is here is this: stereotypically, designers and illustrators are hoarders, collectors of magazines, music, and books; in the digital age, they accumulate JPEGs and bookmarks on their computer screens. We collect for many reasons: for pleasure, the urge for completeness, and for inspiration. But what exactly are we doing when we collect inspiration? German philosopher Walter Benjamin wrote in his much cited work on collecting that every passion lives on the boundary of chaos, but the collector's passion lives at the chaos of memories. Each object in a collection, says Benjamin, is alive with chance and the seeming destiny of the purchase, the moment they came into a life. Almost as if they chose you.

COLLECTING EXPERIENCES

Benjamin developed Baudelaire's idea of the "flâneur," someone who strolls through the city streets, dipping into urban life. The real essence of the flâneur is the drive to collect experiences, perceptions, and atmospheres. The flâneur pulls together a unique, personal storyline from the chaos of life.

What is truly exciting about the contemporary flâneur is that he or she not only generates knowledge, inspiration, and information through accident and chance, but that this knowledge has a visual basis. Listen to Nick Clark's account: "I often find myself rummaging around in junk shops and markets and tacky tourist shops. I do get a little fed up looking through prescribed images on photo-library websites and Google image searches. I'm easily distracted into arcane and eclectic sites or eBay's minefield of things I could buy. I'm drawn toward iconic graphics on packaging, ill-conceived usage instructions, and things that buzz, light up, or spin around." As technology makes it easier for us to filter and organize information, there is a sense that inspiration is to be found in the random.

This page: Some of Nick Clark's collected items and the work they inspired.

LENTICULAR NUNS

What Clark does in his expeditions is cultivate opportunity, disappointment, and excitement. As a creative, he empathizes with the objects and their stories. You could call it imagination, but Clark identifies with these strange objects, their origins, their evolution, their humanity. "I somehow find it reassuring to think that someone at some point thought it was a really good idea to make them. I know there is a lot of obvious kitsch made—like the 'dogs on TV'—but at the same time someone seriously pressed the print button on the 'Gospel Story by Colors' card [from Durham Cathedral in England], or, in keeping with the religious theme, a range of lenticular cards depicting nuns praying in 3D [from an old bookshop in Girona, Spain]. I think it's great that there's a man in Whitstable [in southern England] who makes giant humbugs and a website called Ostriches Online."

These objects are a source of inspiration not because they immediately become a draft, version 1, research. They inspire because Clark gives them autonomy, a life of their own. That's why collecting isn't research. Inspiration doesn't necessarily come from goal-driven research. It comes from having ideas and giving ideas to other things, like objects in junk shops. For creatives, this is especially useful, as their jobs consist of breathing life into client briefs that emerge from highly regulated thinking and branding. In the classical Latin sense of *anima*, creatives animate; they give life—and if they are really good, soul—to a commercial exercise.

CURATORS RATHER
THAN INFORMATION MANAGERS

If there is a lesson in Clark's activity as a flâneur, it is that short-term research is useful, practical, and direct. Under the pressure of deadlines, we often look for something obviously useful, that makes some linear sense, that connects directly with the brief. But there is space for inspiration with deeper roots, that requires seeding and feeding, that emerges quietly over a longer period. Another way of looking at it is that in our research, and in our lives, it's more productive to be curators than to be information managers.

Clark has created this image to demonstrate the relationship between inspiration and professional work—the professional work, the promotional objects, sit beneath the inspirations. It's a shrine to creativity. All of these objects are singular and unrelated, yet they talk to each other, they have a story to tell. Clark sees it as a kind of antidote to screen work. "I think it's because I spend so much time in front of a screen these days, designing things that will inevitably only exist in pixels or vector, that I relish the brief that might lead me to produce something that comes to life off screen." What gives Clark's collection life is not just its physicality, or the passing of some indefinable "spirit," but the way he has transformed his research into an act of curation, and the obvious love he feels for the fabulous diversity in the stories these items express. It's the diversity of expression that makes these objects inspirational.

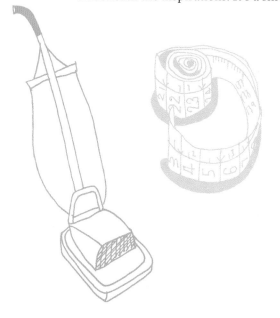

Above: Nick Clark explains, "I picked up this bit of film from a flea market in Spain. It cost one euro. I imagine a child perhaps, looking at its projection, marveling at the process of animation, and being carried away in the spectacular scale and excitement of an airship taking off and crossing the ocean. It reminds me... to see beyond a story... and, if need be, with just a few materials, lines, and colors, create something special."

WHY
NOT TRY...

Visiting a market, garage sale, or thrift store. Don't be considered in your choice of objects, take whatever literally catches your eye. This is about love at first sight. Over time, curate your buys into a collection and explore the relationships and connections between your choices.

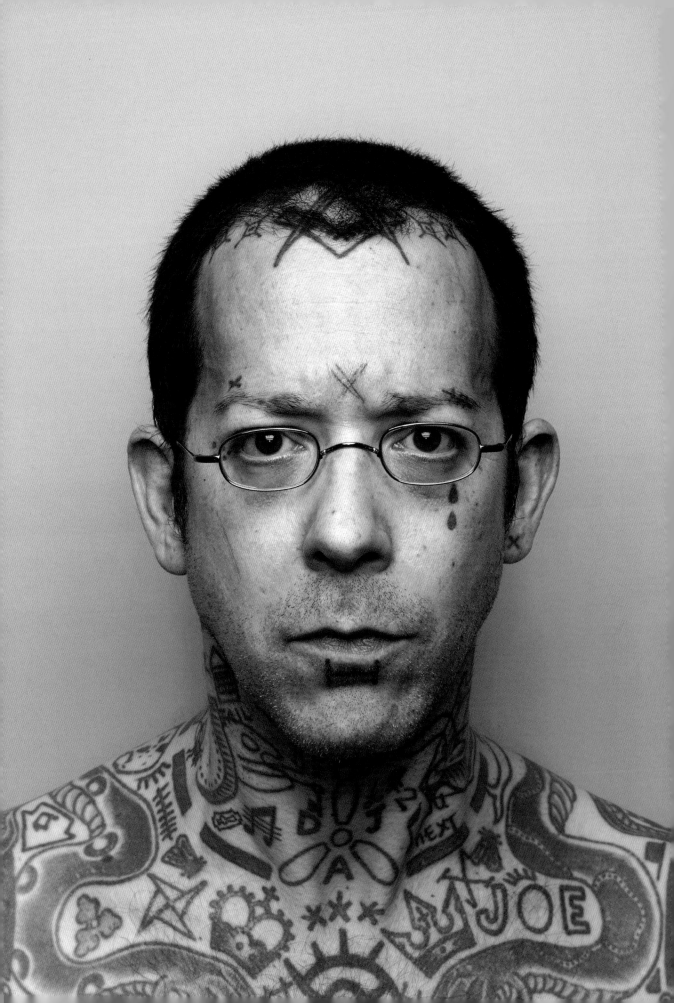

FOUR:
Self-reflection

Me again. Here I am, reading a section intro in a book. Of course, I'm always here, the most consistent part of my life and my practice. I'm always here when I have a great idea, as well as when the clock's ticking loudly and I'm still looking for the right idea. By comparison, the collaborators I team-up with, the books I'm reading, the exhibitions I've just seen, the music I'm listening to, the brief I'm working on—all these things change. My unique personal responses are all I've ever really got, or need, so it's a good idea to know the person I'm working with.

CREATIVE AUTOBIOGRAPHY:
Steve Swingler

What's the first thing you see when you get up? There's the bathroom, the toilet, the mirror, the sink. In the mirror we see a reflection, but at the sink there's a moment of recognition; it's where we catch ourselves thinking. At the end of 1999, graphic designer Steve Swingler got a divorce, quit his job, and sold his house. In 2000, he bought a year-long, round-the-world ticket.

Contrary to convention, Swingler didn't want to find himself. He wanted to "lose" himself, but "to record one piece of recognizable daily life, hold on to one aspect of the mundane, so I didn't lose myself completely." Seeking a constant in a period of change, he took photos of the thing he saw every day. "The constant of something as mundane as a sink intrigues, leads to questions, comparisons, and, for those who have been there, memories richer and more personal than yet another sunset over the Taj Mahal. A sink is a very personal and private thing. Washing in the morning and evening, we take time to reflect. The quotes are all taken from half a dozen or so diaries I kept throughout the trip." The sinks provide a narrative for a life whose story seems unclear.

BATHROOM EXISTENTIALISM

So the Sink project developed. The descriptive tagline runs, "Thoughts and sinks from a year of hotels, hostels, and tents," while the emotive addendum runs, "The mundane will always be there. We should always be somewhere else." Though travel afforded Swingler the opportunity to do this, it's not a travel piece. He says, "I recorded the hotel name, room number, and date so the book could become something of a guidebook," but really it's a work of philosophy. The sink is a framing device. The project is a kind of bathroom existentialism, a collection of the

"I can't go on, I'll go on"—

Samuel Beckett

This page: Steve Swingler photographed every sink he used during a round-the-world trip, recording his thoughts and reactions to events. Swingler says the resulting book "works as a guide to those wishing to follow the same route, but look at the sights, and themselves, a little differently."

Just let it go. It doesn't matter.

Nothing is permanent.

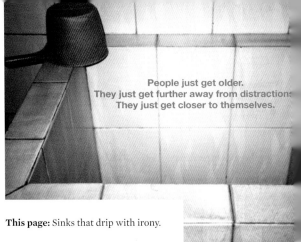

People just get older.
They just get further away from distractions.
They just get closer to themselves.

This page: Sinks that drip with irony.

conversations we might have had with the sink in the morning if the sink had answered back, a series of open-ended beginnings. The sink is where he washes away thoughts like, "Just let it go. It doesn't matter."

The seriality and regularity of the sinks lend the thoughts weight, while their differences—single faucet or twin, running water or turned off, rusty or shiny, but always empty—locate the thoughts in time, place them in the moment. The sink becomes Swingler's theater for playing out self-images, trying on some thoughts, an alter ego modulated slightly from town to town, pushing himself, sometimes downbeat but always keeping going. Capturing more sinks is a way of not stopping. Another town, another sink. As Samuel Beckett said, "I can't go on, I'll go on." The truth of Sink is that truths have to be left behind and rediscovered. "And like that she was gone."

BORROWING YOUR OWN CREATIVITY

The eye that Swingler brings to this project is the same one he brings to his professional work. "Looking at the genuine, everyday realism of the world definitely influences my work," he says. "I work mainly for charities and believe that an authentic approach, carefully targeted, will raise more awareness and money than a purely aesthetic, tricksy advert that may make an impact, but may leave people with the same, cold, 'I've just been sold to' feeling they are treated to by great swathes of advertising and design, of which I am also guilty of producing and being seduced by." And in very literal terms he borrows lines from Sink for headlines and finds it's a window on his imagination for potential clients. "I also look at it and remember how that kind of freedom can open your mind to the 'anything is possible' school of thinking."

But as much as anything else, Sink is representative of a creative process. Swingler is constantly writing songs, poems, and phrases, creating sketchbooks, taking photographs, collecting found objects. "Working through how I think about things, feelings, the world, it's like exercise—the idea of it is a little draining, but once you are into it, you can't think of anything you would rather be doing. These notebooks are raided at creative starts."

WHY NOT TRY...

Finding a private place to meet your self. We don't always have to take a year to get in touch with what we're thinking and feeling, a quality five minutes would do it. We usually meet sinks alone, by the way, as part of a daily routine. We are always at liberty though to arrange a private meeting around lots of other things too—an object, a building, or anything we might normally pass over. The time could be used for writing in-the-moment ideas and feelings, or simply refuelling with information about who we are.

UNCREATING THE SELF-IMAGE:

Matt Willey and Giles Revell

What do we see of ourselves in our photo? What is our self-image? And how inspiring is our professional self-image? These are some of the ideas explored by designer Matt Willey (of Studio8 Design) and photographer Giles Revell in their project Photofit: Self-Portraits, which first appeared in British newspaper *The Guardian* and subsequently developed a life of its own. They tracked down an old piece of police investigative technology—the Photofit kit, first developed by French photographer Jacques Penry and used by police until 1988, when computers took over the job of facial profiling. Willey and Revell then selected a range of subjects who put together an image of themselves with the Photofit kit, and were then photographed by Willey.

The result is a series of diptychs: on one side, a handsomely shot image taken by a professional photographer, and on the other, a self-portrait constructed from a toolkit that enabled police to visualize their suspects. This work interrogates issues not just of self-image, but the idea of portraiture itself, what it can reveal and what it masks, and also the nature of power in the sitter-photographer relationship. Giles Revell writes on his website, "In providing each sitter with the same tools—a 1970s police Photofit kit—the process by which they created their self-portrait was democratized; the immediate, tactile qualities of the kit enabling them to tell their own story as a likeness falls into place, piece by piece."

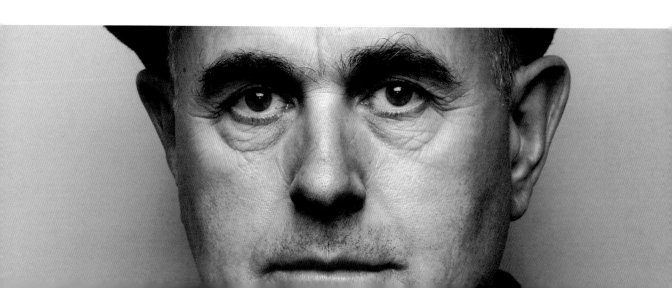

SAY CHEESE

The work plays with our concepts of natural and unnatural. Anne Parry, a police artist, reflects: "I have to admit that I struggled to put together my self-portrait. I smile a lot, so I find it hard to visualize my face looking serious." Criminals never smile.

Most of the subjects in the project were chosen because they had reflected to an unusual degree, for either professional or personal reasons, on issues relating to self-image—a plastic surgeon, a woman with body dysmorphic disorder, a tattooist. In his testimony, portrait painter Humphrey Ocean confesses, "When I do a portrait I always start with the eyes. The heartbeat is in the eye." This belief goes back at least as far as Plato's recounting of the eyes as a window to the soul, and extends to the present day, with designers who know the impact of eye

contact when choosing portraits for the covers of magazines.

The image on the right of each diptych is one created by technology built to discover identity. The one on the left is an image of the self in a moment in time. The Photofit images are a means for the creator to explore his or her own sense of self.

Photofit: Self-Portraits is more than an exploration of an image technology. In the introduction to the piece, Willey and Revell discuss Jacques Penry's 1930s study, which claimed that there was a link between a person's face and their personality, so a philosopher would have highly developed lower cheek muscles (from chin scratching?), while "idiots" would have a receding forehead. Even if we don't believe in Penry's not uncommon linking of personality and

Top left and left: Spreads from Photofit: Self-Portraits, a project by Matt Willey of Studio8 Design and Giles Revell for *The Guardian*, with interviews by Philip Oltermann. Shown here are portraits of Duncan X, a tattooist (top left), and Edmund Davies, a model (left).

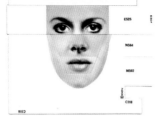

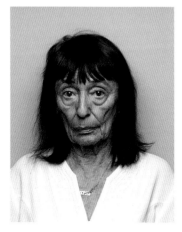
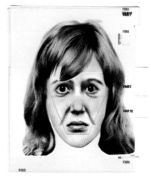

facial structure, many of us still believe that portraits reveal some sort of inner truth, something of our inner selves. Revell and Willey successfully challenge that belief.

Creatives have a sense of self that's a composite self-image—artist, professional, compromiser, idealist, collaborator, individualist—all these different pictures flow into our work in some way. Creatives have to produce a public self-image, brand themselves, so others can quickly "get" who they are, and many spend a large part of their working lives creating this identity. Photofit: Self-Portraits is a compelling exercise in unbranding a self, enabling us to reconsider the underlying assumptions of self-image.

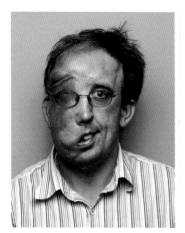
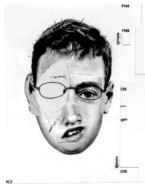

From top to bottom: Portrait of Rajnaara C. Akhtar, a lawyer. Portrait of Beryl Bainbridge, a writer. Portrait of Humphrey Ocean, a portrait painter. Portrait of Marc Crank, a chief executive.

WHY NOT TRY...

Investigating alternative aspects of your creative personality by presenting your brand image in different ways. Will you think about yourself, interact, be responded to, or work differently? How many versions of you are there?

REFRAME YOURSELF:
Tracey Waller

The way a person eats an ice-cream says something about the kind of creative they are. It's impossible to take part in any activity without leaving a creative fingerprint on it. Each time we do something there's a potential for learning something about *how* we do things. These opportunities to witness ourselves, each time from a slightly different perspective, ultimately give us the experience to develop that most crucial of things, our creative voice.

FUNNY FEET

In her own creative practice, Waller works predominantly with the moving image, creating animated films for clients such as Nick Jr, and TV identities and titles for shows such as *Housewife 49* and *Agatha Christie's Miss Marple*, in addition to her personal film work. She's also the course director of the MA in Graphic Design Communication at Chelsea College Of Art & Design in London. She says, "Teaching has been very valuable. It has given me the space to observe, reflect, and talk about the design process, which always feeds back to my own practice and makes me more self-aware of my creative process."

Gaining self-awareness with regard to a creative process can seem like a daunting task. It sounds as though it would require a fully-fledged voyage of discovery rather than a photo of a pair of feet on vacation. Waller started Feet Pictures in the early 1990s on a whim, she didn't set out to make these photos a "project" as such. "It was all very unconsciously done at first, and as the years have gone on and the collection has grown, I have become more conscious and fascinated with the collecting and documenting."

Right: Tracey Waller's feet on vacation.

A DIFFERENT STORY

"As a designer who works with the moving image, I'm interested in narratives. I like the fact [the Feet Pictures] tell a story, and document my journeys from a different perspective." The photos are a journal. They have become a story over time, like frames from a personal movie. Instead of consciously engaging in a project, Waller engaged with herself, and has continued to do so. And her inclination as a result of the continuity of the images was to make a narrative, which is what she does in her creative practice—only this time it comes from a different viewpoint.

Embarking on an adventure with a grand plan isn't necessarily more effective than setting out with no plan at all. Simply being engaged with doing rather than not-doing, having an experience rather than inhibiting an impulse to act or editing an idea at the level of thought, is the process of being creative. The view along the way is noticing what kind of creative you are.

Waller's feet are a bit different, in fact they are a source of friendly mockery, but she still takes them on vacation. Everywhere we go we take ourselves along—warts, imperfect feet, and all. The star of these photos, whether we focus literally on her feet, or instead on the way she has responded to them with her ever-accumulating narrative, is Waller's uniqueness.

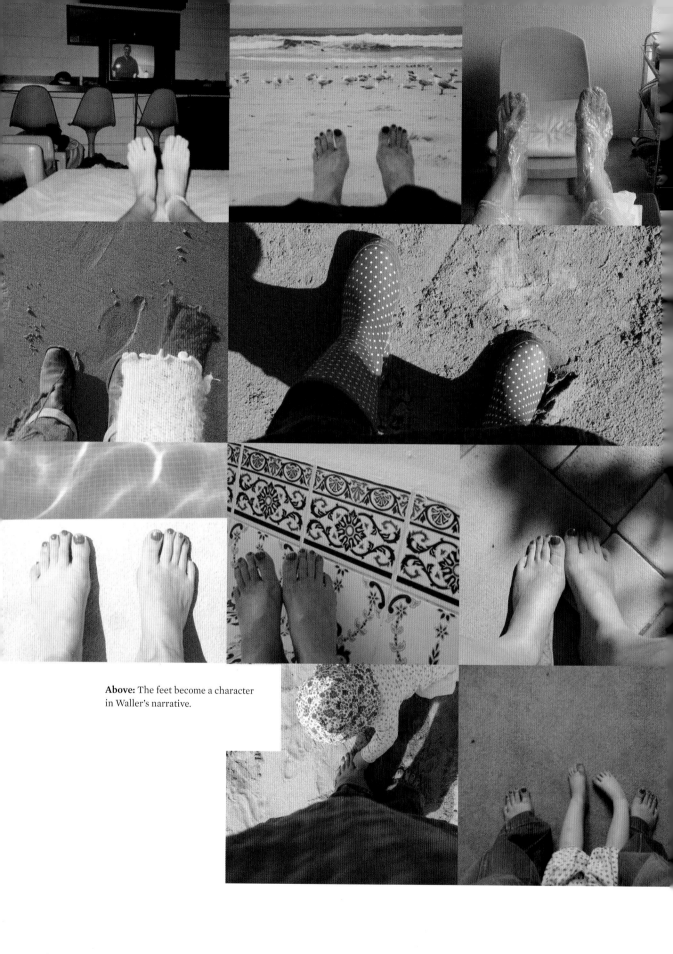

Above: The feet become a character in Waller's narrative.

WHY NOT TRY...

Doing something whenever it occurs to you. Respond to even the faintest impulse to act without any kind of goal whatsoever. You never know where it might take you.

Above: Stills from the live performance of *Constance* at The Wapping Project gallery in London.
Below and above right: The project was also made into a book.

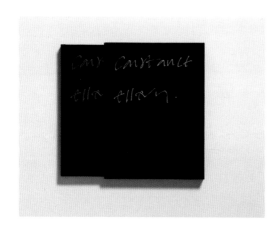

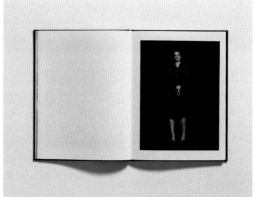

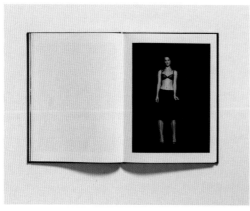

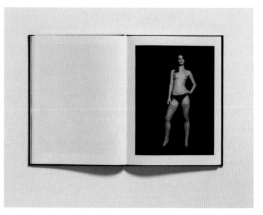

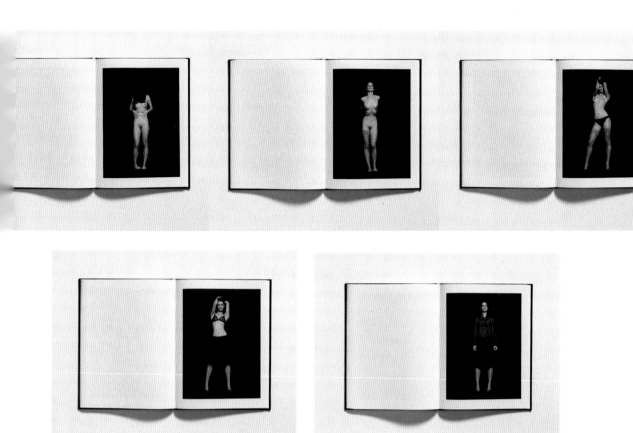

PERFORMANCE:
Jonathan Ellery

Successful creatives are jugglers. They become adept at keeping as many jobs as possible in the air, making sure deadlines don't bump into each other. They are also emotional jugglers—they can't let negative client feedback, or difficult jobs, or a lack of positive response get in the way of doing the job or earning a living.

There is also psychological juggling, which involves balancing ego and humility, single-minded focus and the need to be open to distraction and other possibilities to keep you fresh. A strong ego is often necessary for survival in highly competitive business environments, or for dealing with knockbacks from clients. That's why big egos are a conventional stereotype of the business and advertising worlds—ego is a shell we all need to survive the slings and arrows. But unchecked ego can turn us into human monsters, and into professional creatives who produce functionally efficient work, who take the money and run. Somewhere along the line, great work requires humility and vulnerability.

EMOTIONAL SPACE

Jonathan Ellery, founder of Browns design studio, uses art projects to open up a creative and emotional space for himself, putting himself out there with work that will not be judged by professional criteria. *Constance* was a performance piece he staged at The Wapping Project gallery in London, sparking many thoughts and feelings among an audience that included a mix of people from the art and design worlds.

On one side of a dark basement space—the old pump room, all girders and brickwork, the skeleton of the space—two small stages are lit. On the first, a drummer pounds out a beat, rocking and thumping, building up and slowing down, while on the second stage on the other side of the room, with a chair as the only prop, a young, conservatively dressed woman slowly, deliberately undresses, her face an impassive mask of disapproval. The large crowd stands in the center of this dialogue between drummer and woman. The drumming grinds to a halt. There is a silence, and the woman slowly and deliberately begins dressing again. The whole cycle takes 20 minutes to complete.

SEX AND INTIMACY

"The piece is about my relationship with women," Ellery explains. "My dysfunctional relationship with my mother, my fantastic girlfriends, the female staff in my studio, my ex-wife, good sex, bad sex, all those things come into this fictional character that is Constance. It poses different questions along the way. There are areas that are sexual, and there are areas of gentle intimacy. The drums are doing a completely different thing. If you have got Pearl Jam crunching through when you have a small, lost soul opposite, it's difficult. Or the drums might be very delicate when she is sexualized. It's just my relationship with women."

Those who attended *Constance* would all have their own ideas of what the piece was about, and no doubt some thought that it had nothing to do with design. From the perspective of this book, one thread of what *Constance* was about was, in a very literal way, stripping things back. It was also about vulnerability, not just the vulnerability of the relationships between Ellery and women, but the vulnerability inherent in taking risks, exploring these issues in an unfamiliar language—the language of performance art. It's a space in which Ellery, too, has no clothes. *Constance* teaches us that there is a link between vulnerability and creative ambition.

WHY NOT TRY...

Creatively exploring the personal, psychological stuff we often keep covered up. Getting underneath the day-to-day creative identity we present to the world can put the workaday self in perspective and create the freedom for professional risk-taking. It's true that actions speak louder than words. Show who you are by what it is you really want to do.

 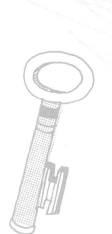 

NOT PLAYING BY THE RULES:

Ellen Tongzhou Zhao

"Even before I've met you, I've already thought and dreamt about you, the reader. This is a rather strange relationship," writes designer Ellen Tongzhou Zhao in her book, *I Am You*, a book about the book, about the book's construction materially and experientially, and about the book's meaning as it is jointly constructed by the creator and the reader. Like the French philosophers and writers it is influenced by, it's a book that explores the conventions and assumptions of book structure, of the beginning and the end, how we read in linear fashion. Zhao writes, "The book will have two beginnings, two ends. From one cover, this book will talk about its structure and how it should be perceived after its conception, the Future. The centerfold is where the book is caught in the moment, the 'present.'" The "present" is highlighted because the present is not a closed moment, it's made up of the pasts that have been experienced, and futures that are anticipated.

I Am You also asks questions about the nature of identity, both of authors and creators, and the identity of books themselves, the stories inside that we demand consistency from. Designers by profession are the gatekeepers of identity and consistency, it's what brands hire them for, to give their story a visual consistency and coherency. There is a grammar of communication that's essential for something to be understood, but equally this grammar is so familiar it allows us to dip out of the moment, out of the communication.

I Am You is a deconstruction of the book's identity, it's a game with its form. "I'm very much interested in and inspired by the transformations of three-dimensional objects and spaces," says Zhao, "because as a graphic designer, I'm somewhat limited by the two-dimensional spaces of the page or the screen."

This page: "The book documents itself," says Zhao, "from conception to production. It highlights the relationship between the book and the reader." *I Am You* is printed by LMGraphie. Photos by Guillaume Boyard.

It's also a way of exploring how meaning is constructed in the moment not just between past and future, but between creator and user. *I Am You* is just one example of Zhao's ongoing interest in what happens in the space of communication. "I try to add extra dimensions or experiences to my work. I try to create an invitation to minimize the spaces between myself and my audience. At the same time, I'm always aware of the impossibility of ever crossing this gap. This need to get closer, to reach out, is what drives me to create." It's about getting close to the person you are communicating with, and the impossibility of closure, because getting close depends on being open. It's

dear ~~cher~~ chère
Mariam
i love j'adore
your sense of humor
i'd like to je voudrais bien
meet you at the park
please write to me at écris-moi à ellen.zhao@web.de
call me at appelle-moi au
+33 (0)6 72 20 32 89 or ou +1 718 478 3364
see the site regarde le site buro-gds.com

ELLEN ZHAO

dear cher ~~chère~~
Jean-Pierre
i love j'adore
your drawings
i'd like to je voudrais bien
visite your studio
please write to me at écris-moi à ellen.zhao@web.de
call me at appelle-moi au
+33 (0)6 72 20 32 89 or ou +1 718 478 3364
see the site regarde le site buro-gds.com

dear cher ~~chère~~
antoine
i love j'adore
tes chaussures
i'd like to je voudrais bien
voir R.B. avec toi
please write to me at écris-moi à ellen.zhao@web.de
call me at appelle-moi au
+33 (0)6 72 20 32 89 or ou +1 718 478 3364
see the site regarde le site buro-gds.com

This page: Business cards that can be filled out "in the moment."

through opening up the codes of how a book is constructed that Zhao changes the expectations of the reader and the reader in the moment. Like her business cards which turn an abstract networking transaction into a communication. And though Zhao is clearly interested in ideas around space, her work is actually about time. Her design rethinks physical space in such a way that it gives her communication direct immediacy. Just like talking directly to you in this instance. Though it's far more sophisticated than simply using the "first-person" voice, it's a lesson that direct communication sometimes requires creative misdirection.

WHY NOT TRY...

Playfully questioning some of the rules of your communication pieces. Though the creative world has long abandoned the office grammar of collars and ties for men, and skirts for women, the grammar of communication too often remains unquestioned. Though clients feel more comfortable with templated communications, there's real pleasure for the audience in work that plays with their expectations. Think of classic Looney Tunes cartoons where the character intrudes on the credits! Clients too often underestimate the innate knowledge of their consumers, and playing with the format can help forge a deeper brand connection.

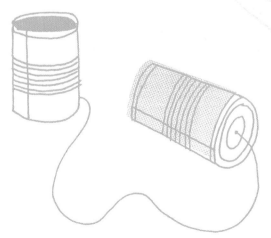

FIVE:
Looking Outwards

Many designers are like moles burrowing away at
the things they make, creating a route for their
ideas to make it through the darkness and then exist
outside in the light, in a world that is separate from
themselves and their familiar dark dwellings. Stepping
out of the shadows, taking broader concerns into
consideration other than the client and their brief
provides an opportunity to see who they are, and who
they are not. It enables a clearer view of their position
in the world. Along with hard-earned exposure for their
graphic achievements, rubbing up against this outside
world offers all kinds of difference, difference that can
be challenging, inspiring, helpful, surprising, exciting,
and ultimately illuminating. What position do you take
in the world?

366x366

For More
e   info@penguincube.c
w   penguincube.com
a   PO Box 113-6117
    Hamra 1103 2100
    Beirut, Lebanon
t   +961 1 74 00 88

COMMUNITY:
Penguin Cube

Collaboration is a buzzword; it's warm and has a glow of equality about it. But collaboration means different things depending on whether you are working with a client, a close colleague, or a two-year old who's spray-painting the kitchen floor. Collaboration means different things to different people. True collaboration is less the dreamy combination of two or more individuals' skills and talents, and more a conversation in which you sometimes realize you are working from different maps and going nowhere fast—but when it works, when it's fun, it's an entirely new creative map. Collaboration involves both pleasure and pain, which also makes it worthwhile and inspiring.

PUBLIC SPHERE

There are parts of the world where collaboration is held in little regard, and where people's lives are put in danger when collaboration is absent from the public sphere. Tammam Yamout, Art Director at Penguin Cube in Beirut, Lebanon, explains, "One of the issues here in the Arab world, in business, is that they don't believe very strongly in teamwork. This is true of a lot of industries, not just design and advertising. People aren't trained in college to work in teams or to build on each other's ideas, and this is a problem we face with some designers and clients we work with. They don't look at it as a collaboration between the client and the design team, but have an engineering mentality—'We are contracting you for xyz.'"

Penguin Cube work within a large and thriving cultural community in Beirut, says Yamout. "Beirut is known throughout the Middle East as the prime location for journalism and for the creative industry. This is because, historically, there are freedom-of-speech laws in Lebanon which are not very apparent in other Arab states."

But the Lebanese business culture is instinctively directive and prescriptive, and many clients don't even pay lip service to collaboration because they don't recognize it as a value. "One of the things we are always trying to promote is the idea of teamwork and collaboration," says Yamout, and so, with Penguin Cube's promotional calendar PiFour, they decided to collaborate with

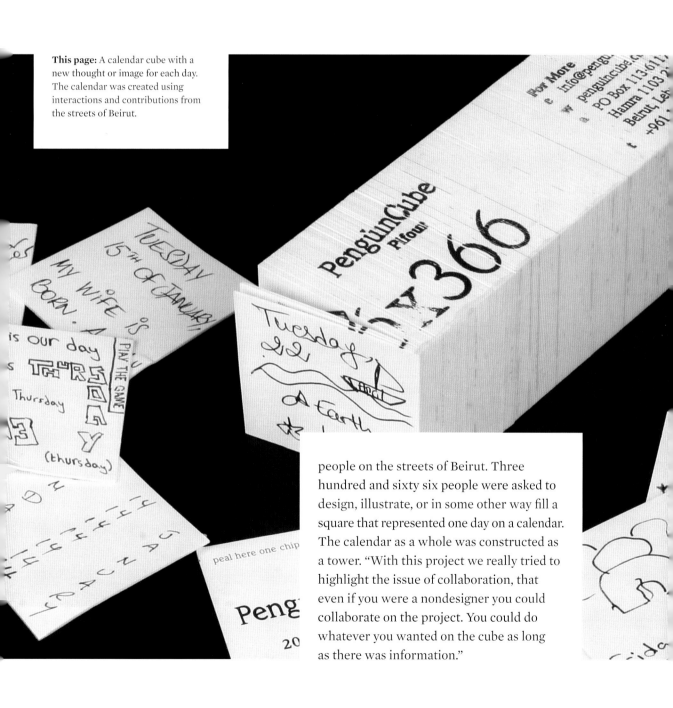

This page: A calendar cube with a new thought or image for each day. The calendar was created using interactions and contributions from the streets of Beirut.

people on the streets of Beirut. Three hundred and sixty six people were asked to design, illustrate, or in some other way fill a square that represented one day on a calendar. The calendar as a whole was constructed as a tower. "With this project we really tried to highlight the issue of collaboration, that even if you were a nondesigner you could collaborate on the project. You could do whatever you wanted on the cube as long as there was information."

Left: A view of the Forgotten Cities hiking trail.

FORGOTTEN CITIES

A lack of cooperation has wide political and human consequences in the Middle East, but collaboration also has many unexpected faces. Penguin Cube were involved in a project called Forgotten Cities, in Aleppo, Syria, in which they helped develop a signage system for a hiking trail that links the sites of ancient cities. The local people mapped the trail for its directions and parameters, and then the villagers produced and mounted the signs.

The project was funded by the Swiss government, who are "trying to generate dialogue between East and West," Yamout explains. "This is to deter extremism, because if you understand the 'other' you are less likely to hate the 'other.' These forgotten cities are early Christian cities, where the Christians tried to fight off the Crusaders— even the Arab Christians tried to fight off the Crusaders. But they failed, and that whole community migrated to the Lebanese mountains. That's why Lebanon is the largest Christian state in the region. These cities show the local community, and the Arabs in the region, that this is where Christianity started. It's not that the Christians are coming to kill all the Muslims or vice versa, actually Christianity started in the Middle East. Once you start understanding your own history, you can start to understand the 'other.'"

MODERN INTERVENTION

The project threw up some unforeseen collaborations with the local community regarding the use of materials for the signage. "There were a lot of challenges with the selection of materials," says Yamout. "If you used metal they would take it for scrap metal. If you used wood they would take the wood and use it to heat up their homes in the winter. We had to use concrete. The Swiss were very happy because they are very big on modern design. It was like a modern intervention on this really traditional landscape. In some of the images you can see the intervention, but you can see that it's not disturbing the landscape, so you can still take a nice photo." The lives and needs of the local community pushed the designers into a solution that was both practical and experimental, and a design that resulted in an unusual collaboration with nature. "The project was very interesting because it plays with a lot of social aspects, it plays with a lot of environmental aspects. You make certain objects which are left in nature."

We will talk more about collaboration in this book. But it's worth remembering that the best collaborations often emerge from the most unlikely sources.

WHY NOT TRY...

Seeking out unlikely and challenging collaborations beyond the professional creative/client space, and looking for feedback on your work outside the usual channels. Professionally, the only time we get responses to our work outside our sphere is through the carefully scripted theater of the focus group. It really is worth seeking out feedback and collaborative projects beyond the usual suspects. You will get fresh, unspun feedback and direction.

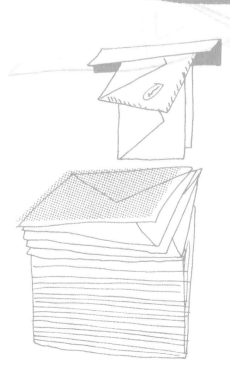

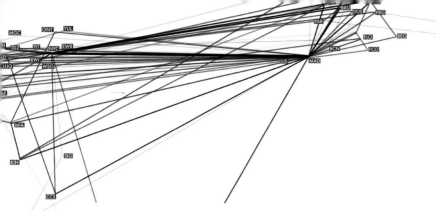

CREATIVE STRATEGY:
Ben Castro and David Catalán

I dea maps are a way of visualizing information that can help us see patterns. Exposure States, a project by Ben Castro and David Catalán, is inspiration visualized as a map. Using their record collections as shared inspiration, they selected 100 records at random. Then they logged where in the world each of the artists and labels were from, and started making the connections. The three letters shown at each point on the map are the first letters of the name of each city. What this map suggests is that inspiration isn't one defining moment, but lots of little important moments that connect to each other.

Castro is part of Madrid-based architectural office Ecosistema Urbano, which specializes in sustainable urban planning. David Catalán is a designer and illustrator, and founder of In Black We Trust, which creates products from recycled waste material. At the core of their creative process is an interrogation of lived experience: "Being exposed to new attitudes, experiences, and information," explains Castro, "is one of the easiest and most direct ways to revisit and expand your own creative world."

RANDOM INSPIRATION

Part of the reason why the two men are drawn to work together is because they operate in different fields and use different approaches; as a result, Exposure States captures a variety of different creative processes. "We decided to work with records for several reasons," says Castro. "Since we are music collectors, they are the main, and often the only 'souvenir' we bring back from any place we visit. They symbolize the process of encoding external data into personal experience. They also emphasize the significance of randomness in creativity. Most of the records we used have no relation to the places they came from, other than the fact that we found them there. They are linked to many other places though, due to the artist origin, record label, or distribution."

Exposure States is a map that appears to schematize creative inspiration, but actually highlights, as Castro says, the random nature of it. Inspiration is more chaotic than we would like to believe. By looking for the one source, the one thing, the big idea that's going to spark it, we can miss out. Though we are sometimes precious about our inspirations, inspiration is nondiscriminatory, we take it where we can find it. Exposure States maps the way that inspiration drinks from many sources.

WHY NOT TRY...

Mapping out some of your inspirations, whether it's books, music, or the work of other designers. Have some fun designing and visualizing the connections between your influences. You may discover hidden patterns among your inspirations and a fuller sense of where you are coming from.

OPPOSITE RULES:
Antidote

Creative companies are employed for their vision—or at least they used to be. Since the advent of desktop publishing in the mid-1980s, the creative options available to designers, and consequently a client's appetite for those options, have been growing steadily. Where once the job of the designer was to deliver solutions, now the job is to give clients as much choice as they demand. This insidious erosion of the designer's authority has clouded the relationship between designer and client and made it more difficult for a designer to construct brave, effective communications that get noticed.

JUST SAY NO

Antidote, an ideas company working in design and advertising, display an immunity to this plight. They retain their authority and use it to communicate clear ideas about important things. Antidote's communications are refreshing because they are not afraid to go against the flow.

Every company wants its message to cut through the media swamp. One way to achieve this is to counter the message that everyone else is shouting. One cry of "No" among a hundred cries of "Yes" stimulates curiosity, at least. When we hear meaningful opposition to what the consensus tells us, it not only affects our view of the subject in question, but—because it previously seemed unthinkable that another viewpoint could be valid—it also gives us the opportunity to reevaluate the status quo as a whole. Like a teenager stepping out of the family home to find their own way of living, the world opens up to new possibilities.

Stating the opposite instead of the obvious isn't always a straightforward process, and being different just for the sake of difference is the most tiresome form of rebellion. For a counterstatement to cut through, it needs to have meaning and relevance. Insight and fresh thinking are required, in contrast to the mindset that simply re-skins what already exists without really questioning it. Sometimes the least-contested messages are those built upon beliefs that are inconsistent with the way people actually live, and miscommunication becomes a bad habit.

A significant amount of Antidote's work is about challenging the status quo. The company (in collaboration with JWT, Michaelides & Bednash, and Digit) created the successful Be My Coach sports campaign, which promoted a surprising positioning for Persil washing powder: "Dirt is good." This is a distinctive statement that trains a wider lens on family life than the one that has always focused in on the ability of a washing powder to get something clean. Every powder does that. One white T-shirt looks very much like another white T-shirt. Clean is boring.

Antidote has also created several projects for the global social-change movement We Are What We Do, as well as establishing its initial brand and website. The first project was a book called *Change the World for a Fiver* that cost just £5 and featured "50 simple actions to change the world and make you feel good." That was followed by other books: *Change the World 9 to 5*, also for We Are What We Do and aiming to inspire change in the workplace; then *Change The World at 35,000ft*, which was created for Virgin Atlantic and offers travelers a chance to make a difference while in the air.

I'M NOT A PLASTIC BAG

For the first action in the first book—decline plastic bags whenever possible—Antidote persuaded Anya Hindmarch to create a desirable alternative to plastic shopping bags. What resulted was I'm NOT a Plastic Bag, a canvas bag that cost £5 and was initially distributed through the UK supermarket chain Sainsbury's. Antidote wrote and designed the line and collaborated with Hindmarch to create what has quickly become a worldwide phenomenon.

These communications don't read like other "green" messages. We've moved a long way from Greenpeace being an isolated voice in the political landscape. Green is now a hot issue, and the subject is normalized by its high profile in the media. Still, the language surrounding the issue is anchored in the need to convince people that climate change is really happening, and also to persuade us that we can do something about it. All this convincing and persuading has a limited level of effectiveness because not everyone wants to do something just because it's the right thing to do. Having to care about an issue like climate change has never been cool, but what Antidote has created with Hindmarch is a cool bag.

The bag speaks for itself. It tells you what it's not. A rebel with a cause, it takes a stand that engenders our support the way an underdog challenger does. This explains the frenzied crowds who have queued for hours at stores, or paid up to US $400 to buy the bag on eBay. There are plenty of well-designed bags on the market that have been created as alternatives to plastic bags, but none has generated such furore.

The tone of We Are What We Do, including the books and bags, is playful, involving, fun. It communicates with a convivial language that is akin to the traditional emotional appeal of advertising. It reframes the language of consumer choice into practical, ethical decision-making. The "we" in We Are What We Do nudges people toward taking ownership of their actions as part of a community of equals, with goals that are achievable.

The bag has its critics. Some have suggested that people just want a cool bag while caring nothing for the environment. Caring, though, is overrated. The world doesn't need people to care more than they do already; instead, it needs people to change their behavior. Likewise the world doesn't need creative agencies that toe the line or get lost in the mire of too many options. We need confident, insightful, courageous communicators who are willing to stand up for a good idea, even if it does initially seem to be the opposite of what was asked for.

Left: Antidote collaborated with Anya Hindmarch to produce I'm NOT a Plastic Bag.

WHY NOT TRY...

Thinking the opposite of whatever you first think, or whatever you're used to thinking. Sometimes it's habit that forms the first response or the desire to act in a particular way. Some of the best ideas in the world stand out because they are counter-culture. Take an idea, take anything, and turn it upside down, inside out, shake it around. Find a truth that no one else has seen.

DO SOMETHING YOU CARE ABOUT:
Mess Hall Press

Graphic design is a service industry, and as such it's possible to take pride in being a professional, doing a good design job, and not care about the social value of the finished product. Graphic designers work at the end of a long process, and on some projects they have to comply with decisions that have been made by others earlier in the process. One way that designers can claim back their creative autonomy is to create projects for themselves and their peers, but this ghettoizes the work and leaves the graphic designer equally disconnected—professionally, at least—from the rest of society.

MENTORING

Scott Pauli wanted more than a bit-part in his career as a designer. He was "really jaded with the entire design world. It seemed to be more about winning awards and making 'cool' stuff, rather than having real meaning." In 2004, after receiving a small grant to teach a teenage design class at a community center with fellow designer Zachary Kaiser, Pauli founded Mess Hall Press, an arts program based at Atwood Community Center on the east side of Madison, Wisconsin. Pauli organizes the classes, is the main contact and mentor for the kids, and handles the program's finances.

The mission of Mess Hall Press is to give children the opportunity to learn from and work with professional designers. Pauli wants "to reach kids that do not already have opportunities in the arts, or are interested and need an alternative to their school curriculum." They focus mainly on high-school students aged 13 to 18, but they've also tried a workshop for younger children, some as young as six, and there are plans to extend this.

Below: Detail of a work-in-progress from the Messy Not Sweaty project.
Right and below right: The designers at Mess Hall Press decided to help with raising funds for a new community skatepark. Each designer paired up with a student to create two custom boards.

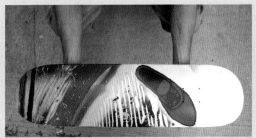

There is a core group of volunteers made up of professional designers, illustrators, and writers, as well as students and graduates of the program: Kevin O'Malley, Zach Kaiser, Heather White, Peter Streicher, Drew Garza, Gerardo Chapa, Tyler Norman, Kevin Johnson, Aaron Davis, and Patrick Masters. Others join this core team on a project-by-project basis. "The other mentors assist with teaching, setting up gallery shows, writing the curriculum and whatever else needs to be done," Pauli explains. "It is definitely a team effort and all of us together make it happen."

This page: The emphasis at Mess Hall Press is on handmade designs, such as these T-shirts and posters, made for the Messy Not Sweaty fund-raising project.

NO COMPUTERS

Due to initial funding limitations, the organization started without computers, so they weren't an option as a creative tool. "But when kids began bringing in projects they had taken home and Photoshopped, the spirit of the work changed," Pauli says. "So we decided to stick with hand-rendered work. We do use the occasional scan or typeface, but the majority is done by hand. It is more immediate and raw. It also gives the volunteers and the students a much-needed break from the computer after a hard day at work or school."

The kids work on projects ranging from T-shirt designs with environmental messages, screenprinting shopping bags for a local farmers' market, and promoting AIDS awareness. For their skateboarding project, the designers at Mess Hall Press decided to help raise funds for a new community skate park. Each designer paired up with a student to create two custom boards. Each team created one board to auction off for the park, and the student was able to keep the other board. All the design and typography is hand-rendered. The techniques include screenprinting, stenciling, painting, and "whatever else the kids are interested in trying." The immediacy of the objects, paints, and inks is more visceral than using a computer, and generates a real sense of spontaneous expression. Pauli says, "They do what feels right to them and design with a great sense of freedom. I almost feel guilty

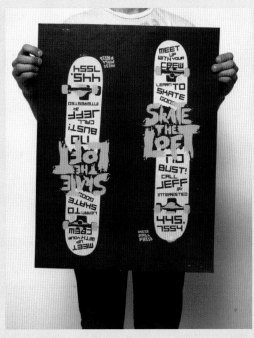

This page: A range of posters created by the members of Mess Hall Press.

Left: An exhibition poster for Mess
Hall Press.
Above: Some of the work shown in
the exhibition.
Above right: Detail of a screenprinted
poster.

sometimes because I learn so much from them and can only hope that I am returning the favor."

Another project involved the mentors "working with the kids to design the identity and interior space of a cafe that is completely run by teens, from marketing and managing to cooking and growing their own organic produce. It has been great so far, and the kids are really into doing a 'real world' project."

Design has the power to be socially binding. Creativity itself is a binding activity and this is particularly true at Mess Hall

Press. It's rewarding to witness our impact on the world. When the kids fall off their hand-rendered skateboards, they hit the ground. When they make a mistake with the paints, it can't be digitally undone. The processes are very direct and real. Actions have consequences. Their world connects together in a tangible way and Pauli has managed to connect his creative process to the creative outcome.

WHY
NOT TRY...

Feeding your talents into your local community. You could promote something you believe in, or start a group of some kind; the possibilities are varied. The process doesn't have to be completely altruistic. Choose something where you benefit creatively as much as the people you're helping. If you work as part of a big media machine, it may be liberating to make yourself part of a smaller community where you can witness the effects of your actions.

FLOWERS OF IDEAS:
Tatiana Arocha

The metaphors we use to describe inspiration and creativity are mostly associated with energy or electricity, such as "getting a spark" or being "fired up." This is such an appealing, powerful idea—one that goes right back to the Greek myth of Prometheus, through to Frankenstein, and is still popular today—that we sometimes forget that inspiration can also come from stillness. We can miss great ideas because we simply don't recognise them in our minds if they're not "Hollywood," they don't come with a sonorous, gravelly voice-over, or with special effects. We pass over them like a quiet, small-budget indie movie.

The movie analogy is an appropriate one for New York-based illustrator, graphic designer, photographer, and director Tatiana Arocha, and her work for The Sundance Channel's THE GREEN series. THE GREEN is a series of programs about the environment and its preservation, intended to create awareness of green issues. This corresponded well with Arocha's own interests "My personal artwork deals with the Colombian rainforest and its preservation," explains Arocha, who is originally from Bogotá, Colombia. "[The Sundance Channel] asked different artists to pitch ideas for small interstitials that had to do with the environment. I pitched the idea of making a piece about rainforest preservation and creating a moment of stillness and peacefulness, a sanctuary." The resulting piece is a simple black-and-white illustration, used as a motion graphic. Quiet. Unspoiled. With its own uncomplicated beauty.

By thinking outside the overheated space of advertising communications, Arocha's piece is powerfully compelling. Her inspirational practice is equally uncontrived—each thought has a voice, none gets preferential treament. "I write down my

Opposite page: Stills from Arocha's intersitial for The Sundance Channel's THE GREEN series..

thoughts. All the ideas I have, I just put them in writing, everything that comes through my head. Then I draw doodles—just motion lines—something that describes a general idea of the composition. I collect images that inspire me. [For this project] I also picked up plants that I saw in the park when walking my dog and then came home and pressed them."

We love the idea of the Big Idea, partly because that often impresses clients. But inspirational ideas don't have to be the loud shouty ones, they can be the quiet wallflowers standing in the corner. Ideas need a mix of inattention to let them grow and a light touch when they finally emerge blinking into the sunlight. Inspiration as a ray of sunshine.

WHY NOT TRY...

Looking through your old project notes and sketches for some of those ideas you've passed over. You may find some that have since grown on you. The root of a good idea doesn't have to come crashing through the window in a Lamborghini. Give the quiet ones a chance.

EXPERTS AND NOVICES:
Graham Fink

Graham Fink is a major figure in the UK advertising industry. He's won countless awards for his work on high-profile accounts such as British Airways, Benson & Hedges, and Silk Cut, and has been voted into D&AD's *Art Direction Book* as one of the 22 best art directors of all time. He worked as art director in various agencies, through to creative director, before becoming a music promos and commercials director in 1995. In 2001, he opened his own creative agency, thefinktank, with partner Deirdre Allen, and in 2005 he became the Creative Director of M&C Saatchi in London.

EXPERTISE IS OVERRATED

It would be understandable to regard Graham Fink as an expert. However, Fink has always viewed the position of "expert" as a trap. He has this adage pinned to his office wall: "For the beginner, there are many possibilities; for the expert, there are very few." Possibilities are the lifeblood of creativity, so the idea of the creative expert is a misnomer.

There's a well-known story: the first advertising job Fink was interviewed for was at CDP, which was then London's top creative agency. He was turned down on the grounds that they were looking for someone with more experience. The next day he returned to the agency dressed up as an older man. They hired him.

Fink's colorful career boasts many comparable anecdotes. This one, though, seems to be at the heart of his attitude toward work and creativity. He never overlooks people because of their lack of experience. In fact, he celebrates the abundance of raw, passionate creativity that so many young people possess. The world of possibilities seen through the eyes of the novice is an inspiration.

FLASH MOB SCHOOL

Passionate about the development of creativity and the rights of novices, Fink created theartschool in 2001. theartschool is part of thefinktank; it is free and available to anyone. Originally the school convened for an afternoon, roughly once a month, in a different location each time. Luminaries from the advertising and creative industries were invited to speak about creativity from various vantage points; speakers have included Gary Oldman, John Hegarty, Peter Souter, Trevor Beattie, William Wray, Luke Williams, Tony Linkson, and Tom Carty, to name but a few. Their brief is to emphasize the creative process rather than a linear, click-through reflection on finished projects. Briefs and creative exercises were set by Fink, as well as the guest speakers, and these would be followed by involving and lively crits.

theartschool was really a "flash" art school (two years before the first official "flash mob" in 2003). Prospective attendees would sign up on thefinktank website and await instructions. Sometimes the venue wasn't secured until the day before the meeting, and attendees didn't know what would happen, or who would be there, apart from Fink. Involvement in an event that had spontaneity at its foundation created a particular kind of excitement. theartshool itself was a novice, a beginner, and was intrinsically creative as a result, so much more so than the colleges and universities where many of the attendees were studying, or had recently graduated from, with their increasingly bureaucratic and stilted approach to (expert) creative education.

Left: Trevor Beattie concludes his talk.
Right: Fink listening to ideas from the students during the first session of theartschool in 2001.

TWO-SECOND DRAWINGS

Society rewards capability, and novices aren't taken as seriously as experts. Opportunities are earned by acquiring status, so creatives need to leave their time as a novice behind if they are to be awarded the best jobs. Professional creatives are under a great deal of pressure to get things right, and being a beginner looks like terrifyingly hard work when each day is filled with uncertainty about how to get things done. It's understandable, then, to want to grab skills as quickly as possible and never look back, but the problem with rushing headlong into the future is that key elements of responsiveness and ability can be left behind. As Picasso said, "Every child is an artist. The problem is how to remain an artist once we grow up."

The creative director of any advertising agency is extremely busy, so time management is of great importance. Fink prioritizes spending time with his teams of young creatives, and actively seeks new people to work with.

Is clutter in the workplace something you

a) take time to straighten up   b) tolerate pr

Would you rather

a) make up your mind quickly   b) pick & ch

Are you more interested in

a) a finished product   b) work in p

Is it preferable mostly to

a) make sure things are arranged   b) just let thi

Are you prone to

a) nailing things down   b) exploring

When finishing a job, do you

a) tie up all the loose ends   b) move on t

Do you usually want things

a) settled & decided   b) just penci

Do you tend to choose

a) rather carefully   b) somewhat

Would you say you are more

a) structured & organised   b) flexible &

Above: The very first session of theartschool. There were no chairs or heating, everyone sat on rugs on the floor with just a few layout pads and some candy. Fink says, "It was the start of something amazing."

"I went to the D&AD New Blood exhibition twice and spent three-and-a-half hours there each time. I loved it. I came out with 30 numbers for interesting people," Fink says. "I saw some quite interesting work on one stand so I called the guy. I asked him questions about his work and he was really flat and uninterested in his own work. I just asked myself, 'Can I really have this guy in my creative department, being all uninterested?'"

The work produced is clearly only part of what's important to Fink. Most importantly, he likes people who know how to use an opportunity when they are offered one. "I met another guy who did these really fast drawings, two at a time, a pen in each hand, which he drew very, very, quickly, like two seconds. They were beautiful. He is coming to work with us. I'm not sure what he's going to do but I'll just get him drawing.

We can make a book or maybe see if what he produces fits with one of our accounts. My mind is just racing at the possibilities!"

Another young creative team who'd attended theartschool attracted Fink's attention. He was impressed by their ideas and gave them a chance of a placement at M&C Saatchi while he was away over Christmas, arranging to meet them when he returned on January 10th to see what they'd been up to. They were essentially left to their own devices. When he got back he found that not only had they managed to obtain a big brief, they'd also written a really good idea for it. Fink immediately got behind them. He offered the brief to director Tony Kaye and the "Smaller Bubbles, Smoother Taste" commercial for Kronenbourg 1664 lager came together. The novices tasted the life of an expert while their world was still full of possibilities.

LOOK AFTER OTHERS

Fink says of his early days as a young advertising creative, "I feel really lucky because I was well looked after. It is so important. When you are looked after as a creative you just grow so much quicker." The factor that sums up that period of being "looked after" was simply the sustained interest of talented senior creatives. Fink and his peers would put work up on the wall and they'd receive good, constructive feedback.

Graham Fink is a passionate creative. He had the vision and nerve to get himself noticed in the first place and was fortunate enough to be surrounded by talented experts who themselves were fortunate enough to spend time with a talented novice. Crucially, Fink has a panoramic view of his position in the creative advertising community.

Beginners have a precious grasp of creativity and a wide-open view of life, something that acquired competence can stifle. There's an exchange to be made. The veteran and the beginner can show each other that the novice is an expert and the expert a novice. Each has something to cultivate in the other, and the dynamic tension inherent in this relationship is a richly creative one.

Top: A packed second session of theartschool, held at the Sculpture Academy in London. Peter Gatley and Tony Linkson took turns speaking. **Bottom:** "Trevor Beattie talking about car ads and how most people don't care. His talk was all about care actually," explains Fink.

WHY NOT TRY...

Spending time with people who are older and others who are younger than you are. The chances are you will learn something valuable whether you're talking to a novice or an expert.

SIX:
Creative Freedom

Imagine the client FROM HELL. "Listen, what I want is this: do anything you want to do, any format, unlimited budget. And one more thing. Did you bring the old brand guidelines with you? Good. We are going to burn them and dance naked around them in our video-conference call with the Chairman." But really how many of us have stared into the abyss given a brief, either professional or personal, that gave us complete "freedom"? The thing is we can never be given freedom, it's not in someone else's gift. We have to take it, commit to it, and shape our freedom in every creative action. Creativity defines our freedom.

STAY LOOSE:
Cormac Hanley

Though we talk about inspiration as a feeling, it is really about seeing, or the activity that enables us to see clearly. Inspiration is a happening rather than a cause, it allows us to arrive at the place we didn't know we wanted to be. And in the creative world, this place isn't just a piece of work; it may be the discovery of a different professional space or a new creative language.

In November 2006, Cormac Hanley, a graphic designer based in Ireland, visited Tokyo, invited by a friend who runs a restaurant and for whom Hanley had done branding work. Hanley had already moved out of Dublin and was in the midst of a change of career, from graphic designer to photographer. He knew he would be on his own in Tokyo for five days while his friend was away on business, so he devised a photography project.

"WHAT CONNECTS TO YOUR SPIRIT?"

Hanley decided to take portraits of people in the street. They would be given a card with three questions: "What makes you happy? What makes you sad? What connects to your spirit?" Hanley explains, "The card explained briefly what I wanted them to do for me, and invited them to answer the three questions in as few words as possible. And ideally it was one-word answers I was looking for because I didn't want the answers to be instantly recognizable. The whole idea of it was much like finding somebody's diary or looking in a magazine, looking at a picture, looking at a face, finding clues." On each of the resulting images are a name and the one-word answers to the three questions. The individuals are urban angels, speaking in shorthand, a language pared down to essentials: vision and idea. "About 60 percent answered," says Hanley. "They took a long time, saying that the questions were very difficult to answer, and very difficult to answer in one word. They thought long and hard. There are perhaps other places in the world where people might say the first three words that came into their heads, but they took it on board that this was like writing a will, or writing an important document, something historical, they couldn't make a mistake with."

This page: "In a mammoth city that lives so fast," remembers Hanley, "the challenge was to break it down into individuals and to try and absorb a little of what they were about."

boy.
world.
self.

beauty.
drunkenness.
punk.

Chihiro
boy.
world
self

Atsushi
beauty.
drunkenness.
punk.

Above: "Some of the images naturally gravitated to one another," says Hanley, "like this one of the fish thrown together and the street portrait of Chihiro and Atsushi."

HARD TO DIG DEEP

The images are very graphic and textural, and very quiet. In some of the juxtapositions you can see Hanley explore the issue of framing, how to give context to a creative decision. Aside from the sheer quality of the work itself, there is a sense in which Hanley is working something out for himself—a philosophy, a new creative language.

"Photographer Chuck Close has a great saying," says Hanley. "Photography is the easiest medium to become proficient in, but the hardest one in which to develop a distinct signature style of your own. I don't know if I'm at, or will ever get to, that point. I really wanted to get outside the comfort zone. I knew that it was going to be terribly difficult to approach people, and the first picture in the entire series is the last that I have on the website. The guy in the park, Toshio, was on a bench, and at first I thought he was a wino, but he had a little bit of English and he explained that he'd had a good job, and his wife had died or something, and his answer was that he'd like to travel. Having broken the ice with him, the cork was out of the bottle and it was easier, but it was very, very hard personally to dig deep and approach someone like that. It's not in my normal make-up."

SURGICAL PROCEDURE

This project did take Hanley out of his comfort zone, and that made it exciting. It's also a transitional project, as Hanley works out what connects him to his creative practice. He sees the transition from design to photography almost as something physical, and the project has helped him reflect on what happens during his creative process. "I used to be an airbrush artist, if I can explain it that way. Much like the camera, the airbrush was a mechanical device—I used to say it tightened up your elbows. If you were an artist painting with a big brush and getting messy with the oils, you'd be very loose and you'd be splashing the paint onto a canvas and it wouldn't really matter. Working with an airbrush was the opposite of that, almost like a surgical procedure, to the extent where you'd be nearly holding your breath when you were operating it. So I think that project was an elbow-loosening exercise. With commercial work or studio work or still life, you're tightening up constantly and you need something that's going to get you away from obsessing over the minutiae of a shot."

This page: In these short portrait exchanges, Hanley noted that you cannot simply "take" someone's picture—they have to "give" it to you.

"KEEP GOING!"

Hanley is talking about capturing the bigger picture, and that applies equally to an individual image and to the wider choices you make in your work. He continues, "I had two to three minutes with each person to try and make a little bit of contact, find a location, worry about light, take the shot, then let them go. You were just going to do the best you could in that little window, and yet it wasn't photojournalism. You were directing but you really had to be satisfied with what you could do. That's something that I carried back to the other work. If you are obsessing too much, you are going to miss the point—you won't be looking for that contact. If you fix the model's hair 15 times and then look through the lens at the hair and not the model, then all is lost anyway."

The project title, Ganbatte, came from one of the subjects in his photos, Ryota. Walking away after the shot, Ryota "turned back to me, smiling, raised his fist to the air and called out 'Ganbatte!'"—which Hanley says is a "rallying cry to the spirit, to keep going, to never give up."

There is real strength in this work. It depicts a certain kind of human courage that helps sustain us, helps us keep going when things don't have that clarity.

This page: Hanley says "Being an outsider you can experience some amazing cultural contrasts; a city so safe that a woman can fall asleep on the subway. Where puppies are for sale outside brothels, perhaps to tempt businessmen to take them home to the kids. Amazing."

WHY NOT TRY...

Putting yourself in a situation you don't normally feel comfortable with, and plan a creative project around it. It gives you "creative armor" and the resulting project can help clarify ideas or career decisions. Deep down, no matter how sceptical we are, we all believe in a kind of "creative destiny." This sense of destiny keeps us going when things are hard, it allows us to keep believing in our talent, but it can also stop us from seeing other creative possibilities for ourselves. We are not Jedi warriors, we really don't have to keep on facing our daily Darth Vader in the form of clients or work we don't like. We really can remake our professional future.

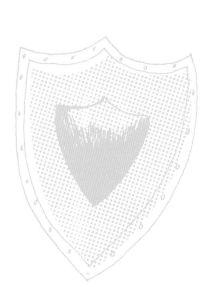

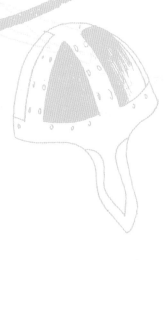

DRIFT:
Jim Chambers

The most important task for a communication designer is to find a way to present information in a fresh and original way. See things differently, then show others how you've seen them. Sounds simple, but the time constraints of a commercial outfit place this process under a great deal of pressure, so the familiar groove worn by habitual creative practice grows ever deeper. Frameworks and structures are reassuring, so making a deliberate move—physically or psychologically—to see things from a different perspective is an act of courage.

French philosopher and Situationist Guy Debord urged his readers to revisit the way they looked at the world, particularly urban spaces. One of the strategies he used was called the *dérive* (sometimes translated as "drift"): a walk, usually through city streets, with no particular goal or purpose in mind. Debord was passionate about jolting people out of predictable, well-trodden paths and into new and autonomous experiences.

WALK MAN

Jim Chambers, graphic designer and art director, is acutely aware of the value of drifting. In his personal project Walk Man, he carried his camera around for a month while listening to music on headphones. Fuelled by his interest in the synchronicity of apparently random events, Chambers made a personal document of the collisions between his choices of music and his location. His aim was to create a record of the "music video" going on in his head. The photographs were taken randomly while the lyric sung at that moment was noted in a book. The songs were played in shuffle mode to add another level of randomness to the concoction. The process is like putting a paper clip around the various layers of his experience at that moment, filing them for future reference, and by ultimately presenting the two components in the

This page: Image from Jim Chambers' Walk Man project. Chambers explains: "When I walk around with my iPod headphones in my ears, whatever I see becomes my own personal pop video to the music playing in my head."

i love myself
better than you

you want her
you can't have her

and
we
were
gone

into
the
trees

familiar square format of CD or album artwork he has created a neat piece of packaging for a personal moment in time. For Chambers, however, one of the key aspects of Walk Man is to see other people interpret the random pieces and ascribe meaning to them. He explains, "It's an absolute joy to have done this project because it makes the viewer look for meanings, connections, and explanations where there aren't any. Perhaps this is the purpose of the work—to make the viewer think, feel, and use their imagination."

There's an investment, too, in Chambers practicing his own ability to think, feel, and use his imagination outside the studio as well as in it: "I see it as the fuel to my regular job. If I'm being creative elsewhere then it can only benefit the day-to-day stuff."

rule britannia
is out of bounds

This spread: Images from Walk Man. Chambers describes the project as "A juxtaposition of image and words—both random, yet connected. But when the picture and lyrics are combined, it's impossible not to look for a connection."

it lives
marry me

i'm trying
i'm trying
i'm trying
i'm trying
i'm trying
i'm trying
i'm trying

With the proliferation of devices that enable us to experience all kinds of media while on the move, many of us have had a tangible experience of multiple layers of information hitting us simultaneously. Reading a book while on a train journey, hearing an argument at the end of the carriage that can be heard over the song on the headphones. The chances for exciting alignments of events are rife.

WHY
NOT TRY...

Finding your own way of noting or recording your sensory experiences. Go for a walk. Take a camera, a notebook, a dictaphone, or just your own wide-open eyes and ears. You can do something with the results once you get back to where you came from. It's always worth trying something out creatively, throwing a few things together. No matter how good an imagination a person has, there's no substitute for actual experience. Keep moving.

CREATIVE BODY:
Ingo Fast

Inspiration gives us a new direction, a new map, and finding a new direction sometimes demands that we throw ourselves into an unfamiliar space to discover where we are going, or need to go. Inspiration is also sometimes a matter of rediscovering ourselves physically. At work, we surround ourselves with accessories, tools, research, or ambient stuff—all of which can shelter us and blur our creative focus when we rely on it too much. We navigate our digital desktops and hook ourselves up to all the devices we buy to make our work easier. But we can also begin to lose the ability to locate ourselves, our thinking, beyond the screen in physical space. In the 1950s, French philosopher Maurice Merleau-Ponty began to rebalance the tradition of thought that separated mind and body, arguing that we have a bodily intelligence; we experience and perceive with our body. Merleau-Ponty was merely the first, and philosophers, psychologists, and educationalists increasingly agree with the idea that intelligence is embodied. Yet in the professional space, creativity, inspiration, and ideas are still largely conceived as happening solely in the mind.

BRAIN EMBOLISM

German-born illustrator Ingo Fast had long carried a desire to go on an extended journey, and when he suffered a brain embolism while diving in 1999, he decided he needed to make it happen. He would work while he was on the road. Eventually, in September 2005, Fast left his New York home and started traveling, jetting between Antigua, Rio de Janeiro, Hanoi, Hong Kong, Sydney, Palau, and Hawaii. After a one-month hiatus in April 2006, he set off on a second journey around the world. This time he would take it slow. He started with a boat across the Atlantic. Then bus. Ferry. Hitchhiking. Car. Train. Horse. Motorcycle. River boat. Container ship. And a flight between Indonesia and Australia. It was as much an exploration as a journey, a kind of physical mapmaking. Fast had always enjoyed creating illustrated maps, the closest link to his love of traveling, "because that way I can temporarily drift off into

imagining I can see the world from a bird's-eye perspective, relieving that feeling of constantly having ants in my pants, wanting to hit the road."

Fast pared himself down to the essentials. "No notes to read through, no bills to take care of or calls to reply to that weren't directly related to work, no dozens of alluring distractions lingering on my desk at home, easily cluttered with magazines, books, unopened letters, and ephemera I couldn't bring myself to hide quickly enough before it would take over my space. I forced myself to boil down the tools I needed to work to the most essential ones: laptop, scanner, paper, pens and pencils, cables, and a few adaptors. Plus communication tools like a satellite phone or VOIP adaptor."

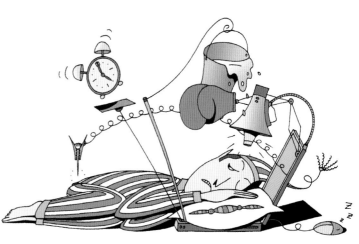

This spread and following page:
The freshness of Fast's illustrations have the air of breaking news bulletins. Each image parcels out time; the work shows someone literally using their creative tools to "collect" their thoughts.

ABLE-BODIED

Fast had to create and file a weekly and bi-monthly assignment while on the road. Forced to adapt, he stopped using watercolors, using digital coloring instead, and quickly learned the art of ad libbing when faced with "falling from a horse in Mongolia with my laptop and scanner strapped to my back, torrential rain knocking out the satellite signal for the only internet connection on a Malaysian island, and a remote earthquake cutting off most internet connections in all of South East Asia." Fast became a very able-bodied improvisation artist.

Fast has brought back with him inspiration for a different form of mapping. "What I learned to do much more easily during my travels was to keep a thought or an aspect of a place or a situation in a sketch. I have pages filled with writings and sketches. Now I feel I pay more attention to the small details I see around me, whether I travel or just walk the streets of the city I live in, and I tend to make more of an effort to document my life photographically." The journey, as you can see from the sketches, turned Fast into his own recording device.

The images are on-the-spot news from his imagination; he became his own desktop-publishing system, search engine, and library. "While many of the things we surround ourselves with are certainly beautiful to look at, inspirational, and also offer us a sense of security," says Fast, "while traveling I realized that I didn't really need so many of these things, and rather than reading up on stuff, I could draw more significant inspiration from real life, from a myriad of surprising aspects in all the cultures I was allowed to get a glimpse of, and from what I heard and learned directly from others."

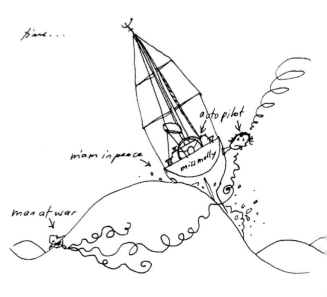

WHY NOT TRY...

Thinking of your own physicality as a source of inspiration, a "machine" for recording or gathering information. As creatives we spend so much time in our heads, at our desks, we miss the opportunity that simple physical presence affords us. Go for a run, a walk, a cycle, a swim; note the physical impact on your body, see what it's responding to and what your mind begins to respond to in the environment surrounding you.

INSPIRATION, COLLAGE, AND THE COLLECTIVE:
Lucha Design

Somewhere in between working on your own and working for a company there is "the collective." The collective is a more fluid working experience. On their website Lucha Design describe themselves as "an independent collective of creative professionals based in New York. We understand and respect critical thinking, research, and the creative process." In this arrangement the creative boundaries between your work and the group's work are always shifting and self-reflection becomes essential in establishing and opening up boundaries. And discovering these boundaries sometimes entails diving in at the deep end.

Lucha Design is made up of Agnieszka Morawska, Russell Austin, and Luis Bravo, and their music video *Sunrise* for the band Yeasayer was their collective leap in the dark. "We wanted to kick ourselves in the ass," they say. "We felt like we would learn by throwing ourselves into the deep end of the pool. The thought process went something like... 'what would scare the hell out of us and what would be the most challenging, insane thing to undertake... an animated music video, perfect!'"

The project was an aesthetic and organizational collage. "There is something amazing about how things recombine and morph into something new once you take some scissors to it," say Lucha explaining *Sunrise*. "We are obsessed with collage and design is really a collage artform. We are always piecing things together, so we thought this world we created should really be this mad mash-up of textures and images recombined to create a new context."

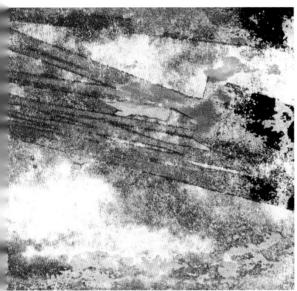

HOW TO BE
UNFINISHED

Collage is the art of diverting intentions.
You are taking somebody else's work and its
intended meaning and resituating it in an
entirely different place. Collage as a work
is always unfinished, it's about being
unfinished, which fits with the way Lucha's
members say they inspire each other: "We
have created a good environment where
we are able to just blurt out our most insane
ideas and not get laughed at. Like the blues
or jazz we build upon a piece of an idea. In
the end it is a mixture or collage of a stream
of consciousness; an improv session. And
beer... beer and cigarettes. They have
ideas in them. If you eat them you will
get ideas, too!"

This page: Images and process
elements from the music video
Sunrise for the band Yeasayer. "We
used an array of visual techniques,"
say Lucha, "surfaces and textures
were built using Polaroid transfers,
background characters were made
of cut paper and collage."

Collage is about multiple perspectives, just like the astronaut shown here constructed from multiple TV screens, a heroic image as a collective experience of different perspectives. "If you do not look at things like everyone else you start thinking about how to use them in a different way," say Lucha. "Just look at something upside down. See. It looks like something else. Now you can use it. We talk a lot about running and swimming and yoga … so eventually we will stop smoking cigarettes and get ideas from sweating." Inspiration in a collective is about the freedom and emotional security to jump into the strangeness of each others' imaginations.

This page: Collage is the technology of the multiple-perspective. Why have one pair of eyes when you can have as many as you need?

WHY
NOT TRY...

Taking a pair of scissors to your most familiar creative routines. Once they're in pieces, discard the bits you want to leave behind, invent some new bits or borrow them from colleagues, then put it all back together again in a way that feels fresh, even if at first it seems scary.

this

SECRET WEAPON

will give more POWER *to* *your*

LITTLE SOLDIER

LINZIE

SEVEN:
Playing Around

Game on. Jump in and fly that car that's sprouted wings and evade the sofa-sized bumblebee. Hit FIRE! Cook the politicians who promise to fund the arts but are covertly made of cake, go, zoom over the asteroid field and beyond the rainbow where there's a big juicy sitting-duck of an idea just waiting to be plucked by the player determined to have the highest score in dogged pursuit of a killer solution. Reload.

The most successful designers take creativity very seriously; however, without serious fuel-injected fun to hypercharge the creative tank, it's game over.

PLAY TIME:
I Saw It First

Being creative is a fundamentally uplifting experience, partly because the process of coaxing out an idea is very much like playing. There's a stage in a creative project that's simply about gathering information—intellectual, emotional, and sensual; a process that's comparable to a child's investigation of a new toy. It involves turning things upside down, inside out, shaking them around, and importantly, to imagine and reimagine them: can this book be a hat instead?

Play and creativity are intrinsically linked, and because play is so often seen as something to be earned, something that comes after hard work, this link has caused confusion about the significance of creativity. Schools for young children have historically underestimated the importance of creativity, reducing both play and creativity to superfluous treats rather than key parts of the curriculum. Many of us will recognize the experience of being rewarded for our academic efforts with access to art sessions, and conversely, our lack of motivation along with other bad behavior being punished by its withdrawal. The cost of judging creativity as less important than other aspects of learning is not only the lack of developed artistic skills, but of the confidence to use play as a valid and useful part of life. In a feature on play in *The New York Times*, Stuart Brown, president of the National Institute for Play in California, said: "If you look at what produces learning and memory and well-being, play is as fundamental as any other aspect of life, including sleep and dreams."

Left: Packs of the Cover Up "stunt" covers.
Right and following page: Stickers from the Wake Me Up At set, for use on the London Underground.

GET YOURSELF A REAL JOB

The cliché about artistic professions not being a "real" job is a drag. The way artists work is a variable activity which sometimes doesn't look very much like "work" at all (especially when it involves playing and having fun), even though there are other times—in production, for example—when the hours needed to execute an idea to a high standard grow longer and longer.

Alice Tonge and Cathy Hutton are advertising creatives who understand the creative dynamic between hard graft and having fun. In addition to their work at 4Creative on campaigns for UK broadcaster Channel 4, British Airways, and Persil, they've created a small business called I Saw It First, making "inventive products that make you smile," as Hutton describes them.

Their products are funny. Wake Me Up At is the "underground sticker set" that's designed for use on the London Underground. Cover Up is a kit for enabling fun while hiding it from the world at large. There's a choice of two "stunt" covers for use while reading trashy material in public: *Complete Japanese (Masterclass Edition)* and *Advanced Quantum Physics (Difficult Edition)*.

SERIOUS WORK

These projects are designed to support guilty pleasures—and there's no guiltier pleasure than enjoying a great idea! The ideas aren't just funny, they are also deeply mischievous, and probably naughty enough to be deserving of an art-class ban and some extra math.

The name I Saw It First conjures up an image of excitable school children, competitively rushing to find the next great thing and claim ownership of it. Hutton says, "We were just having a drink after work, catching up and having the usual banter. We generally come out with random stuff when we chat. Some friends like to just catch up; we tend to do that first, then hit on a subject matter, pull out our notepads, and get scrawling."

Tonge and Hutton obviously love their work and their collaboration, moving from the studio to a bar only to start throwing ideas around as part of their downtime. It's a good idea to use the energy of a friendship to get creative. A good brainstorming session can fly when it's fuelled by lively energy, trust, and mutual encouragement. A bad brainstorm is a dry and frustrating affair that's often caused by a premature "No" in one form or another that prevents or stifles the build-up of flowing creative energy.

The I Saw It First ideas are initially the product of a good time, but that's not the whole story. As soon as Tonge and Hutton hit on the ideas they liked, it was time to get serious about making them. "We were flat-out almost every weekend. We worked so hard getting our sticker pack just right. There were numerous designs, legal issues with the TFL [Transport for London], not to mention sourcing the right printer, getting in the materials, and costing it all up."

Tonge and Hutton funded the first product with their own money. They say, "We currently don't make any profit from what we do. We reinvest the money made from each product into the next project. Because we fit everything around our jobs, getting stuff into production and into the shops can be a slow process. But it's a great thing to do with your mate, particularly when you're both passionate about ideas."

Being a working creative is an art in itself. It's important to have the guts to do whatever gets the job done best, regardless of how little the work resembles "real" work. The challenge is how to take creativity seriously even when it's funny, and not to doubt the results of a job that's involved giggling over a friendly drink instead of slaving over a hot computer.

WHY NOT TRY...

Doing a brainstorm every two weeks. Make it part of a dinner party or some other kind of social gathering, it doesn't matter as long as kicking ideas around is at the heart of the interaction. There doesn't need to be a goal beyond that of stretching your creative muscles—that and having fun! Choose a few subjects, an object in your lives or a system you use, and riff on how you could do it better. See what it's like to remove all seriousness from the process and allow the ideas to go off the client-scale and into areas you may generally avoid during day-to-day studio time.

CUSTOMIZING AND RECYCLING:

Peter Chadwick

Confident creatives acquire a bold personal vision about their projects. They get inside the subject matter, get to know it, and then take the client on a journey. One creative's dream job is another's nightmare, and because even the most established design studios aren't always able to choose which briefs come through the door, professionals need to be able to build a meaningful relationship with their project, regardless of what it is.

TAKING OWNERSHIP

The first thing many people do when they acquire a generic, mass-produced object is to somehow make it unique and personal, thereby taking ownership of it. Whether the mark of the owner is an embroidered initial on a handkerchief or flames roaring across the side of a pimped-up car, making something unmistakably "mine" is a rite of passage.

This process of acquiring, or (in the case of a brief) being given something, and then assimilating it is a fundamentally creative act: having the freedom to interpret things differently; seeing something the way nobody else sees it; renovating a used object, simply by reevaluating it; humanizing the brand spanking new by making it intimate.

Children do this naturally. It's one of those priceless things that we all did at one point in our lives, and then to varying degrees have managed to unlearn. To give us adults our due respect, children do this partly through the bliss of ignorance, whereas once the object is known and understood, it is a conscious exercise to remember it can still have another life.

This page: Pop about pop. Chadwick's company, Popular, works in the vernacular of pop culture, where expensive commercial design is often beautifully defaced and reworked by teenagers. It's why in the world of pop culture, customization is the sincerest form of flattery. You make an object of love your own. Creativity as an act of worship.

GET YOUR HANDS DIRTY

Art director and founder of Popular, Peter Chadwick makes a significant amount of personal work in which his primary aim is to "get his hands dirty" by working with three-dimensional objects and photography, specifically excluding his computer from the process because he uses it so much to create work for his clients. His personal work is often a revision of something he admires. Like a DJ remixing the world around him, Chadwick sees something, likes it, and proceeds to create his own version of it, taking his admiration as a point of departure.

Ghetto Blaster and Guitar are part of an ongoing series called Music To My Eyes. Chadwick says, "One of my favorite ever record sleeves is Malcolm McLaren's *Duck Rock*. That was the inspiration for the first piece in this series, Ghetto Blaster, and after it was completed I decided to work with different musical instruments."

The *Duck Rock* sleeve is an exuberant montage. In the center is a ghetto blaster with cow horns growing out of the sides. The record's title is sprayed onto the speakers, and antenna jut out in various directions, suspending words and headphones.

The exuberance of Chadwick's Ghetto Blaster is certainly in line with the *Duck Rock* sleeve, but there's something very different about it too. Ghetto Blaster is more sophisticated and more reverent. The bright and playful colors sit against black, like a child's toy removed from its original environment and placed carefully on display. The black space is a protective area, resembling a barrier in an art gallery. This is Chadwick's ghetto blaster, not McLaren's, make no mistake.

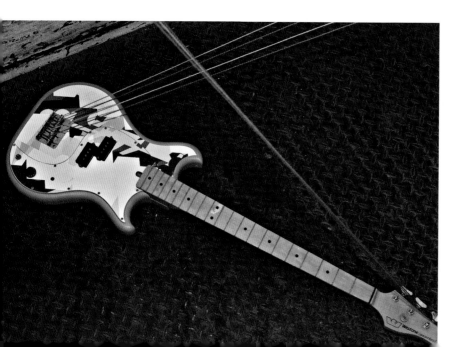

This spread: Chadwick's pop sculpture demystifies the fetish objects of pop. Pop is about the image and Chadwick's work breaks that "fourth wall," the guitar strings really are material objects.

COLORED FLARES

In another project, Paintball, Chadwick explains that, "While watching one of my favorite movies, *Apocalypse Now*, there's an amazing visual scene where they set off colored flares in the boat. This was the initial point of reference and inspiration for this project. We developed it into doing the shoot on a paintball site with colored flares used in the background."

The point of this project is not to make a duplicate of another's work, but to have a fuller experience of (in this case) the movie clip, and then take the story somewhere else.

Chadwick is open to changes of direction during the creative course of these projects, something that can be more restricted when working with a client. Collaboration is important too, and adds a different voice that can affect the progress of the piece. "I decide on a concept/

Above: Still from Paintball, a project inspired by *Apocalypse Now*.

direction for each piece, at which point I commission another preeminent creative such as an illustrator or photographer to work on it with me."

This flexibility and openness is partly what is so intriguing about Chadwick's work and about the creative process itself. The curiosity about what happens next, when the mist has cleared, is what creates the impetus to move forward.

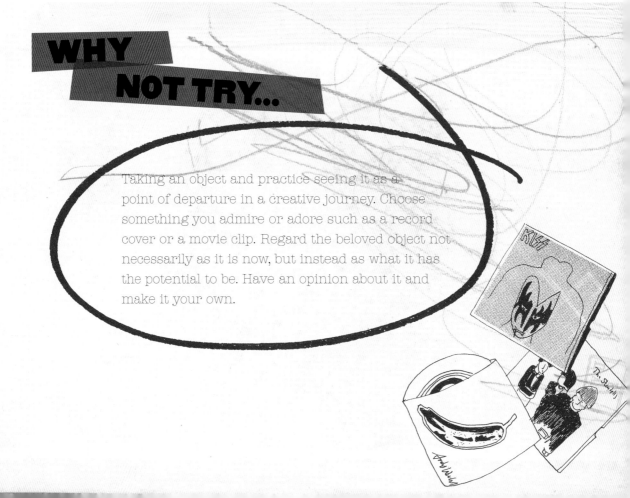

WHY NOT TRY...

Taking an object and practice seeing it as a point of departure in a creative journey. Choose something you admire or adore such as a record cover or a movie clip. Regard the beloved object not necessarily as it is now, but instead as what it has the potential to be. Have an opinion about it and make it your own.

CUSTOMIZING AND RECYCLING:
Hjärta Smärta

At Swedish design company Hjärta Smärta they run regular non-client workshops for themselves, preying on the found object, stripping away its expected meanings and creating something surprising. "We tend to use readymade things and put them into a new context," they explain. "To put the right things in the wrong place is something we have always enjoyed."

Shoe Diary is Hjärta Smärta's contribution to an exchange project called Civic Matters in which American, Finnish, and Swedish artists and designers met in Los Angeles for two weeks of seminars and workshops. Each day, a pair of white leather women's shoes was customized as a response to what happened that day and to thoughts about LA in general.

Another project, Neon Letters is the result of a workshop in which found neon signs were converted into a new typographic system. While Ice Cream Marbling is just that: different ice-cream flavors used to create marbling effects similar to those used in classic book designs.

"We like to give the client something unexpected that wasn't asked for in the brief, something that makes the work feel like a gift. Something they never knew

they needed until they got it. Since we regularly have our own projects and workshops, we have a supply of 'extra' ideas that sometimes turn out to be a good match with a client's needs."

Exercising that most childlike of abilities, to see things afresh, is crucial to all of these projects. Having the imagination to represent things in a new and unexpected way enables you to pause and take stock. In a speedy world so saturated by visual messages, the ability to refresh something we've grown blind to really is a skill worth revisiting.

This page: Using "found objects" such as ice-cream is an art of opportunity.

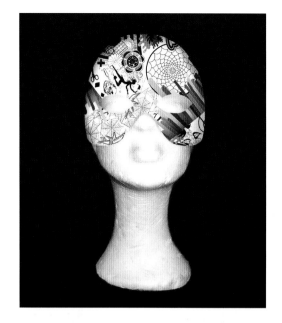

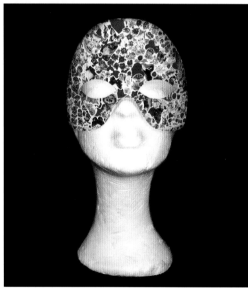

Left, top and bottom: These masks are self-portraits of Angela Tillman Sperandio and Samira Bouabana, the founders of Hjärta Smärta.
Top right: Neon Letters, a new typographic system made from found neon signs.
Below right: Examples from Shoe Diary, Hjärta Smärta's contribution to the Civic Matters exchange project.

WHY NOT TRY...

Making a reservoir of extra ideas that have the potential to be a good match with your client's needs. Hit the ground running with every client project with the riches of your reservoir in mind. Starting from a position of abundance (of ideas, of confidence in acquiring more ideas, and then of consequential high self-esteem) is easier than working a way out of a sense of emptiness.

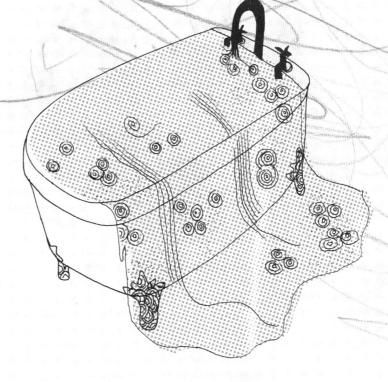

POWER, IMAGINATION, CONTEXT:
Thonik

As a designer all your relationships with clients are defined by power. They have it, you don't. He who pays the piper calls the tune. What the designer has is the power to create the tune, the power of imagination, the ability to generate meanings and connections. Yet often, deep down, we can be intensely frustrated by the power relationship with clients, and it's because when they reject work they don't connect with the story we have created for them or their brands, whether that's through a logo, an ident, a title sequence, or a website. And the challenge for us is to keep a sense of our own story going as professionals when our creative and professional judgment is constantly being interrogated.

It's why pulling together your own work, for a portfolio or a showcase, is an incredibly useful exercise in reflecting on your creative evolution, an opportunity to use your past work as inspiration. It gives you an opportunity to take back the power of recreating your own story. Which is what Dutch design agency Thonik did. In 2006 Thonik designed the communications and catalog for *China Contemporary*, an exhibition of Chinese avant-garde architecture, art, graphic design, and fashion, held in the Nederlands Fotomuseum in Rotterdam. This project led to Thonik being invited back to China to showcase a retrospective of their work at the Shanghai Art Museum in 2008.

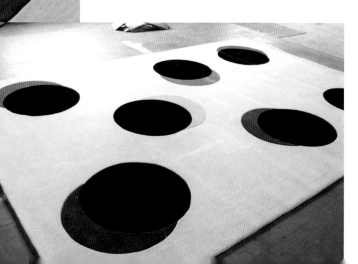

This spread: This installation of 16 carpets, based on existing Thonik designs, was first shown at the Shanghai Art Museum, followed by a show at the International Architecture Biennale in Venice.

TYPES OF POWER

The title of the show given by the Chinese curators was *Power,* as the theme captured the work the studio had done for various local libraries (sources of cultural power), for local authorities and the Dutch Socialist Party (sources of political power), and the posters that the studio had created for the Silver Jubilee of Beatrix, Queen of the Netherlands. But truly all retrospectives have the theme of power because the retrospective is an examination of the powerful ideas and work that have sustained a career.

The challenge for Thonik was to get inspired to go beyond a simple representation of their work. "We have seldom seen an exhibition in which new, interesting images are made with the aid of printed matter," say Thonik. "Although we couldn't get away from display cases, which we designed ourselves, we wanted our work in this museum context to have a new expressive power all of its own. The challenge here was to translate essentially worthless printed matter into something valuable and unique."

In the end they settled on something that was integral to the exhibition venue and that expressed local cultural power: they put their designs on carpets. "We decided to do an installation with hand-knotted woollen carpets," say Thonik. "One of the reasons for this is that an old carpet culture still exists in China and at the moment the avant-garde is taking an interest in it. In our own culture carpets have been associated with prestige, status, and power for centuries. The carpet is more than an adornment in the residences of queens and emperors; in the past, people hung carpets from the windows of their houses to welcome the monarch as he made his state entry into the city." Carpets have symbolic power, but what Thonik did is give a functional object creative power and also make the gallery visitor rethink the nature of what design is. Is it simply a pattern? A graphic? Design is clearly more than that.

TAKING BACK THE SPACE

Thonik used their imagination to challenge the conventions of the gallery retrospective—a format which can neutralize the meaning of work. They also used their design skills to defuse the symbolic power of the gallery space, the "white cube," in order to take control of telling their own story in the way they wanted. As art critic Brian O'Doherty argues in *Inside the White Cube*, "The ideal gallery subtracts from the artwork all cues that interfere with the fact that it is 'art.' The work is isolated from everything that would detract from its evaluation of itself. This gives the space a presence possessed by other spaces where conventions are preserved through the repetition of a closed system of values....the sanctity of the church, the formality of the courtroom, the mystique of the experimental laboratory..."

Because of what they do designers are attuned to fitting ideas to different contexts, whether that's the format of their work, the brand, or the audience. That's what makes the creative challenge, but sometimes it's important to take back the context, the space in which your work is shown so you can give it back its communicative power. Enabling the work to tell its own story allows you to understand your own.

Below: Installing the Thonik exhibition at the Shanghai Art Museum.

WHY NOT TRY...

Reframing your portfolio and recreating it as a project, as grafitti, as a lightshow, or as an installation. We package up our creativity in entirely appropriate professional ways, it's how we pay respect to the formalities of getting work. Yet our creativity is also inappropriate because it challenges convention, power, and the commercial relationships that define the day-to-day. Have some fun exploring the deeper creativity of your portfolio in an unconventional fashion, and see what it reveals.

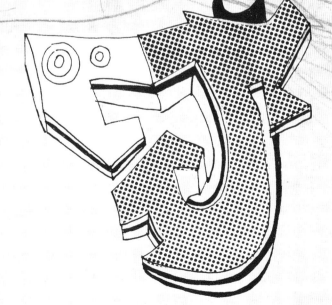

JUNK CREATIVITY:
Linzie Hunter

Dear close personal friend, read this book and not only will it change your life, but if you recommend it to five of your friends, your sex drive will improve and you'll make millions! THIS REALLY WORKS! Spam is advertising written by 12-year-old schoolboys. In very literal terms it's junk. Your email package will recognize it as "junk mail." Junk food has no nutritional value. Junk is waste. In *The Naked Lunch* William Burroughs says that junk is the ultimate form of merchandise because the seller doesn't sell the product to the consumer, he sells the consumer to the product. What's more says Burroughs, the seller doesn't develop the product, make it more sophisticated, he simplifies and degrades his customer. OK, so Burroughs is talking about heroin, but the same pattern applies to junk communications. All junk communications degrade and simplify the client.

SPAM CONNOISSEURS

Yet the creative eye can redeem junk, can inject creativity into it, and give it value. Connoisseurs of spam have emerged. Lee Ranaldo of Sonic Youth has written a volume of poetry inspired by spam, and there are websites showcasing "spam Dadaism," a form that emerged to bypass sophisticated text filters, introducing random literary references among its logorrhoea. But the most poignant and delicate work inspired by spam is that of illustrator Linzie Hunter.

Hunter explains, "I didn't plan out the project at all. It came about because I was interested in doing some more lettering work, something that I had done as part of illustration jobs but not exclusively as a lettering artist. For a while I'd been saving spam emails that made me laugh into a separate folder in my inbox—not for any particular purpose, really. I'm just a hoarder, I suppose. Anyways, I just decided to use some of them as text for some lettering exercises—firstly, 'No More Lonely Nights for Linzie.' I guess I have a self-deprecating sense of humor. The spam I selected were ones that just made me laugh, mostly the more insulting ones."

Right and below: Lessons in communication 101. The medium is the message as Hunter's illustrations turn junk into folk art.

RECYCLING JUNK

This is recycling junk, turning information waste into treasure. Hunter's work is a true act of creativity, transforming the ugly and meaningless into something glowing with innocence, beauty, and naivety. As much as anything else her illustration is about a transformation in tone that changes the message and gives it humor. Did all spam prove inspirational and susceptible to flowering creativity? "Some worked better than others," says Hunter. "But I found that in some ways the color and lettering style wrote itself. Sometimes it was choosing a style of lettering that totally contradicted the message, which would make something that might be a bit distasteful, less so." For example, the subject line "No more lonely nights" made Hunter think of "a huge billboard-type announcement, like old Hollywood." And "Local chicks who need lovin' on the side" suggested "Hicksville/small-town trailer trash—so I went folksy with a shape and pattern that made me think of a diner apron." And though this is the only work that seems to explicitly reference cooking and domesticity of a sort, the appeal of Hunter's work lies in its upbeat domestic positivity. She turns ugly, mindless sales pitches into cheery mottos, an effect partly achieved by a highly textural illustration style that at times looks as if it's sewn on.

This page: Hunter's illustrations are also about the imaginary persona behind the message. Each piece has a singular appeal, with a character-based choice of style and color, making each illustration into a little design drama.

CULTURE JAMMING

The unlikely consequences of Hunter's work mirrored the unlikely nature of its content. Posted on Flickr, it grew virally until it was picked up by *Wired* magazine and website Boing Boing, and then an interview in *The New York Times* was read by an editor at publisher Chronicle Books, which led to a postcard book. Professionally, all this has taken Hunter in a specific direction: "Interestingly I've spent most of this year working on just lettering-based projects, mostly book covers and advertising work. Usually the commissioners have referenced the spam work, even though not all the commissions have a direct relation to the work's content." Perhaps the most unusual and inspired commission was an illustration for a healthcare book for teenage girls, commissioned after the art director saw the spam project and the image with the line

"From now on your small breasts need not be the cause of your embarrassment."

Among the many brilliant things about this work—the creative decision-making, the execution, the humor—is the micro-revolt by Hunter. It's a domestic version of culture jamming, but without the grandstanding. It's a lowercase revolution. And it makes you think of the inspirational possibilities inherent in the stuff that surrounds us. When Mies van der Rohe said "God is in the details," he suggested that we pay too much attention to the big picture and miss the potential in the minutiae of everyday life. For creatives, this is partly a result of the pressure of work, and partly a result of clients who think and deal in marketing abstractions rather than the real daily lives of human beings.

It's about attending to those things the French philosophers of the 1960s and 70s called "the marginal"—the unimportant, the insignificant, the email that even the email software judges is junk. And the irony is that the marginal is often central to our lives, but is also the thing we're running away from. What Hunter has done is develop an ecology of creativity, a modern version of alchemy, an act of conversion. God is in the emails.

WHY NOT TRY...

Keeping an eye on the things you routinely throw out. What makes one thing worth keeping and another thing worthless? Have some fun taking the unwanted thing out of its context, and redesigning it in entirely inappropriate ways.

CREATIVE STRATEGIES

MAKE PERSONAL CREATIVE COMMITMENTS AND KEEP TO THEM.

GIVE YOURSELF SOME STRUCTURE. MAKE YOUR OWN RULES.

PHOTOGRAPH SOMETHING DIFFERENTLY.

PRAISE YOURSELF. SELF-CONFIDENCE CREATES OPPORTUNITY.

CLOSE YOUR EMAIL APPLICATION.

GET THE IDEA OUT, MAKE IT, AND THEN SEE WHAT YOU THINK.

TRY THE OPPOSITE OF WHATEVER SEEMS COOL.

LOVE YOUR MISTAKES.

ASK LOTS OF QUESTIONS.

SIMPLIFY. CONCENTRATE ON WHAT'S ESSENTIAL.

EXERCISE YOUR BODY.

TAKE A BREAK, EVEN IF YOU DON'T HAVE TIME FOR ONE.

RISK SPONTANEITY.

DO A SKETCH OF YOUR CREATIVITY AS IT IS RIGHT NOW.

EXPERIMENT WITH WORKING AT DIFFERENT PACES. MAKE QUICKLY. MAKE SLOWLY.

PLAY AT WORK.

TAKE YOUR CREATIVITY
SERIOUSLY.

CUT IT OUT. MAKE SPACE
FOR SOMETHING ELSE.

DON'T BE PRECIOUS
ABOUT IDEAS. CREATIVITY
DOESN'T HAVE AN END.

SUSPEND JUDGEMENT.
FOLLOW YOUR INSTINCT
WHEREVER IT WANTS
TO GO.

KEEP YOURSELF WELL FED.

TREAT BAD IDEAS GENTLY
SO THE GOOD ONES KNOW
IT'S SAFE TO SHOW
THEMSELVES.

TALK TO PEOPLE.
SOCIAL INTERACTION
BREEDS IDEAS.

DO IT BEFORE YOU TALK
ABOUT IT.

BE AUDACIOUS.

SHARE WHAT YOU KNOW.

BE REALLY SELFISH.

MAKE SPACE FOR YOUR
CREATIVITY AWAY FROM
YOUR WORK.

WHEN SOMEONE YOU
KNOW MAKES SOMETHING
AMAZING, GET MOTIVATED
RATHER THAN BITTER.

FEATURED DESIGNERS

Alfalfa Studio
www.alfalfastudio.com

Antidote
www.antidote.co.uk

Ben Castro
www.basurama.org

Cormac Hanley
www.monomondo.com

Cuartopiso
www.cuartopiso.com

David Catalán, In Black We Trust
www.inblackwetrust.com

Ellen Tongzhou Zhao
www.buro-gds.com

Giles Revell
www.gilesrevell.com

Graham Fink
www.thefinktank.com

Hjärta Smärta
www.hjartasmarta.se

Ian Lynam
www.ianlynam.com

Ingo Fast
www.ingofast.com

I Saw It First
www.isawitfirst.co.uk

Jim Chambers
jwchambers@btinternet.com

Joel Armstrong
www.absolutearts.com/portfolios/
j/jarmstrong

Jonathan Ellery
www.jonathanellery.com

Linzie Hunter
www.linziehunter.co.uk

Lizzie Ridout
www.lizzieridout.com
www.artsparklets.co.uk

Lucha Design
www.luchadesign.com

Mark Gardner, Imaginary Forces
www.imaginaryforces.com

MasonBaronet
www.masonbaronet.com

Matt Willey, Studio8 Design
www.studio8design.co.uk

Mess Hall Press
www.messhallpress.org

MWM Creative
www.mwmcreative.co.uk

Nick Clark
www.nickclarkdesign.co.uk

Noah Scalin
www.alrdesign.com

Penguin Cube
www.penguincube.com

Peter Chadwick, Popular
www.popularuk.com

Robin Rimbaud/Scanner
www.scannerdot.com

Sophie Beard
www.sophiebeard.com

Stefan G. Bucher, 344 Design
www.344design.com
www.dailymonster.com

Steve Swingler
www.steveswingler.com

Studio AND
www.and.ch

Tatiana Arocha
www.tatianaarocha.com

Thonik
www.thonik.nl

Tracey Waller
tracey@studiotrace.com

INDEX

ACKNOWLEDGMENTS

Thanks to all the contributors whose work was truly inspiring. To Brian Eno and Peter Schmidt's *Oblique Strategies* which inspired our own less oblique ones and to the writings of Adam Phillips, Lewis Hyde, and Haruki Murakami who helped us think a little quicker and run a little faster.

Page 21: Extract from Wislawa Szymborska's Nobel Lecture © The Nobel Foundation 1996.

Page 32: Extract from *Screening the Beats: Media Culture and the Beat Sensibility* by David Sterritt © 2004 by David Sterritt; reprinted by permission of Southern Illinois University Press.

Pages 34–36: Images © MMVII Lions Gate Television Inc. All Rights Reserved.
Production company: Imaginary Forces (IF).
IF Directors: Mark Gardner, Steve Fuller. IF Executive Producer: Maribeth Phillips. IF Producer: Cara McKenney. IF Coordinator: Michele Watkins.
IF Designers: Jeremy Cox, Fabian Tejeda, Joey Salim.
IF Animators: Fabian Tejada, Jason Goodman, Jeremy Cox, Jordan Sariego. IF Editor: Caleb Woods. Client: AMC. Studio: Lionsgate. Production Company: U.R.O.K. Productions. Director: Alan Taylor. Executive Producer: Matthew Weiner. Producer: Scott Hornbacher, Bobby Williams (Lionsgate). Post Production Supervisor: Todd London. Editor: Malcolm Jamieson. Editorial Company: Encore Hollywood. Music Composer: RJD2 "A Beautiful Mine". Date released/Aired (Day/Month/Year): 7/19/07.

Pages 62–66: All images contained within Homeward Bound copyright the British Library or Lizzie Ridout unless otherwise stated.

Pages 72–74: *World Musical Instruments* Publisher: The Pepin Press BV; Series editor: Pepin Van Roojen; Editorial co-ordinator: Kevin Haworth; Preface: Bart Hopkin.

Pages 94–95: Photos by John Ross (book stills).

Pages 98–99: Photos by Guillaume Boyard.

Pages 114–119: Photos by Tyler Norman.

Page 160: Shoe Diary photos by Martin Nicolausson, Tom Eriksson.

Page 164: Extract from *Inside the White Cube* by Brian O'Doherty courtesy of The University of California Press.

Pages 166–168: Prints: Le Prints from 20x200.com; Posters from Thumbtackpress.com; Postcard book published by Chronicle Books.